SOUTHERN AFRICAN
BIRDS
A Photographic Guide

Ian Sinclair

STRUIK

To my daughter, Kiera

Front cover photograph: Red Bishop (W.G. McIlleron)
Title page photograph: White Pelican (H. von Hörsten)

Struik Publishers
(a member of The Struik Group (Pty) Ltd)
Cornelis Struik House
80 McKenzie Street
Cape Town 8001

Reg. no.: 54/00965/07

First published in 1990
Second impression 1992
Third impression 1993

Text © Ian Sinclair 1990
Photographs © the individual photographers 1990
Illustrations © Struik Publishers 1990
Maps © Struik Publishers 1990

Concept design by Jenny Camons
Page design and artwork by Tracey Carstens
Typesetting by McManus Bros (Pty) Ltd, Cape Town
Reproduction by Fotoplate (Pty) Ltd, Cape Town
Printed and bound by Kyodo Printing Co (Singapore) Pte Ltd

ISBN 0 86977 794 7

Contents

Introduction 4

How to use this book 5

Species accounts 6

Birding etiquette 139

Glossary of terms 140

Further reading 142

Index 143

Introduction

In the past few years bird-watching, or 'birding' as it is now commonly referred to, has become one of the fastest developing pastimes throughout the western world. To accommodate this rapid development, a wide range of books has become available, covering most aspects of the topic but with field guides predominating. So why then yet another guide to birds?

In the area that comprises the ornithological region of southern Africa (that is, the area south of the Zambezi and Cunene Rivers), nearly 900 species of birds are known to occur. However, as almost two-thirds of the species in this area are not common, have specialized habitat requirements, are extremely furtive and are thus difficult to find, or are virtually impossible to identify correctly unless one has years of experience, it is highly unlikely that one would see all these species. Many other species are only vagrants and have occurred fewer than five times and the chances of seeing these are remote. This leaves only a few hundred species that are seen frequently by the casual or novice birder.

This book has been designed with this in mind: the 260 species selected are not necessarily the most common in southern Africa but they are the conspicuous birds and thus likely to be encountered most frequently. These are the birds that you can expect to see on a day trip to the coast, or in a nature or game reserve. By using this book in the field you should be able to identify the bird you have seen or be able to deduce to which family the bird belongs and then later to identify the bird at home, using more comprehensive books.

One of the main attractions of birding is that birds are a highly visual and appealing subject and they occur in virtually all habitats. Although most birds are very visible and many are abundant, it is not always that easy to identify them correctly. Familiarize yourself with the different species that appear in the plates by leafing through the book when you have a spare moment so that you will be able to recognize a species the first time you see it in the wild. Most of the birds in the book are easily recognizable in the wild but there are a few that require more skill to identify.

Frequently a bird is not clearly seen, is seen only for a short period, or a feature on the bird may become exaggerated, possibly resulting in a misidentification. Avoid snap identifications: rather aim for sustained and better viewing to identify the bird. When confronted with a bird that is not instantly recognizable, first judge its size, then try to work out its general shape, colour pattern, the length of its tail, shape of its wings and every other detail which might be conspicuous. Often there is one striking feature that is sufficient to distinguish the bird, but sometimes it takes the combination of several features to make a positive identification.

In theory, the most satisfactory way to be certain of an identification is to photograph the bird and then, at your leisure, identify the bird from the photograph by consulting books or by showing the photograph to an expert. This may sound feasible but, in practice, the prohibitive costs of photographic equipment notwithstanding, taking the photograph requires a considerable amount of skill. A far better idea is to use a notebook and pencil and to jot down details of the bird you are watching and to make a rudimentary sketch showing the obvious features. From your notes and sketches the bird should be relatively easy to identify at a later stage.

Much has been written about the equipment necessary for birding and many of the books listed in the section on Further Reading contain sufficient detail to help you decide which binoculars, telescope, tape recorder and so on will best suit your purposes. There is also a book which suggests where and when to go birding in southern Africa. Many courses on bird identification are offered by different clubs, societies and universities and these will all help to hone your skills in the field. There is, however, no substitute for first-hand observation and the longer you spend in the field improving your abilities in the correct identification of birds, the greater will be your understanding of birds in general.

How to use this book

This book has been designed with clarity and ease of use in mind. The species' descriptions are succinct, with key identification pointers emphasized in *italic type*. Where necessary, photographs show both male and female to highlight plumage differences, and illustrate breeding and non-breeding dress, as well as adult and immature birds. The length of the bird (from bill tip to outstretched tail) is given, except in the case of the Ostrich whose measurement indicates its height. The call is mentioned only if it is characteristic of the bird. In each case, an up-to-date map has been provided to reflect the known distribution of the species. Birds that are similar in size, shape and colour – and are thus likely to be confused – are grouped for purposes of comparison. The thumbnail silhouettes are intended to guide you to the family of birds most closely resembling the bird you have seen, as you flick through the book.

A habitat map showing the various vegetation zones mentioned in the text, a glossary of birding terms, as well as a diagram showing the parts of a bird, are featured on pages 140 and 141.

Abbreviations and symbols used in this book

ad. = adult   imm. = immature
br. = breeding   non-br. = non-breeding
♂ = male   ♀ = female

Ostrich Height 2 m

Male

Unmistakable: the *tallest and largest* bird in the region. The male has contrasting black and white plumage, a rufous tail, and a reddish front to the legs when breeding. The female and imm. are drab brown and white. Very young bird might be mistaken for a korhaan but has flattened bill, thick legs and is fluffy in appearance. Outside game reserves most birds are either domesticated or feral. A nocturnal loud booming is the call given by the male. Found in extreme desert conditions, open plains and bushveld.

Jackass Penguin 60 cm

Adult   Immature

The *black and white face pattern* on this small penguin is diagnostic. The general *upright stance* and black and white plumage render it unmistakable when seen ashore. At sea it swims very low in the water with only the neck and head breaking the surface. Imm. is a dark greyish-blue and lacks the head pattern of the ad. When travelling fast through water, it 'porpoises' at regular intervals. The loud, donkey-like braying call is given mostly at night. Most common on the south and west coasts where it breeds on off-shore islands.

Dabchick 20 cm

Breeding   Non-breeding

 One of the *smallest aquatic birds* in the region. *Sides of head are chestnut* during breeding season (diagnostic). Non-breeding birds are drab greyish-brown; in all plumages, a pale spot at the base of the bill is diagnostic. In flight the Dabchick has very rapid wing beats and shows a white wing stripe and a bright white belly. Frequently dives; often will emerge with just the head showing to watch intruder. Call is a high-pitched, whinnying trill. Frequents freshwater areas with emergent vegetation.

Blackbrowed Albatross 90 cm

Adult resembles a large Kelp Gull with much longer, straighter wings. Ad. has *white underwing with very broad black borders* and this, combined with a yellowish, orange-tipped bill, is diagnostic. Imm. has predominantly *dark underwing with a grey, black-tipped bill*, smoky smudges on head and an incomplete greyish collar. Sometimes ventures close inshore along the southern and western Cape coasts.

Adult   Sub-adult

Yellownosed Albatross 80 cm

Adult   Immature

 Smaller and more slender than Blackbrowed Albatross and has *white underwing narrowly bordered with black.* The bill appears totally black but at close range a *yellow stripe is evident on the upper ridge.* Imm. has underwing similar to that of ad. but lacks yellow on bill and has a totally white head, lacking the grey wash on head of ad. Much more abundant on east coast and follows sardine run along Natal coast during winter.

Pintado Petrel 40 cm

An easily identifiable, conspicuous seabird. The *chequered black and white upperparts* are diagnostic; the underparts are predominantly white with a dark throat. Flight very floppy for a seabird but, in stronger winds, it glides and turns, twisting from side to side. Does not venture close to shore except during storms but is common around fishing boats.

Whitechinned Petrel 54 cm

J C SINCLAIR

 Considerably larger than Sooty Shearwater, is much *darker brown, appearing almost black*, and lacks silvery underwing. Diagnostic *pale bill and white chin* can be seen at close range. Wings long and narrow; has a towering, careening flight action high above waves. Regularly ventures close inshore around the coast and frequently follows fishing trawlers. Normally silent but will utter a fast 'titititit' when alarmed.

A WILSON

Sooty Shearwater 46 cm

J C SINCLAIR

 Smaller and paler than Whitechinned Petrel and has diagnostic *silvery underwing*. Flight is swift and direct with rapid wing beats interspersed with glides when bird banks over waves and flashes its silvery underwings. On migration, very large concentrations of these birds come close inshore along the western Cape coast. They feed in mixed flocks with Cape Gannets and Cape Cormorants.

9

Broadbilled Prion 30 cm

Prions are notoriously difficult to identify in the field but this is the prion most commonly encountered around the coast. Features common to all prions are the blue-grey upperparts with an open 'W' across the back and wings, a dark-tipped tail and white underparts. On this species the particularly *broad and heavy-looking bill* is diagnostic. Sometimes occurs in large numbers; in adverse weather many are beach wrecked.

White Pelican 180 cm

Adult   Immature

This large bird can be confused only with the smaller Pinkbacked Pelican but the ad. is much *whiter and has contrasting black flight feathers and a brighter yellow pouch*. Imm. is much larger and a darker brown than imm. Pinkbacked Pelican. Frequently flies in 'V' formation. Groups feed by herding shoals of fish and then scooping them up in their large bills. The only pelican in the Cape coastal area.

Pinkbacked Pelican 140 cm

A. WEAVING

Noticeably *smaller than White Pelican* and a much *drabber greyish colour*; never as crisply white. The flight feathers do not contrast strongly with greyish wings and body and in flight the *underwings appear uniform* in colour. The bill pouch is grey or pink, not yellow as in White Pelican. Imm. is darker than ad. but never as dark brown as imm. White Pelican. More inclined to feed solitarily than White Pelican. Occurrence is virtually restricted to Natal where it frequents coastal estuaries and freshwater lakes.

Cape Gannet 85 cm

G. CUBITT

Above: adult
Right: immature

Differs from the large albatrosses by being *whiter, having a long, dagger-shaped bill and a long, pointed tail*. Imm. is dark brown version of ad. and differs from Whitechinned Petrel by *fine speckling on back*, its pale belly and much larger size. When feeding, plunges into sea from considerable height with partly folded wings. Seen regularly from shore in all weathers, sometimes as it gathers in large feeding flocks.

P.R.B STEYN

Whitebreasted Cormorant 90 cm

Adult   Immature

By far the *largest of the cormorants*. Has a *clear white breast and throat* and, in the breeding season, *white thigh patches*. Imm. has variable amount of white on breast and belly and is best distinguished from Reed Cormorant by its much larger size. Differs from similarly sized Darter by having a much thicker neck, broader head and shorter tail. Coastal birds avoid feeding over the open ocean, preferring sheltered bays and estuaries.

Cape Cormorant 65 cm

Adult   Immature

The *most abundant marine cormorant* of the region. Sometimes vast numbers can be seen from the shore as they fly in straight lines or skeins to and from their feeding areas. Ad. is a glossy, bluish black with a conspicuous orange throat patch. Imm. is a dowdy brownish colour and lacks the white underparts of the larger Whitebreasted Cormorant. Feeds actively on anchovy and sardine shoals, leap-frogging over each other in pursuit of food.

Reed Cormorant 52 cm

Adult   Immature

B RYAN   J J BROOKS

 Most often seen in association with Whitebreasted Cormorant and Darter from which it is distinguished by being much smaller. Ad. in breeding plumage has a barred back, *orange face and throat*, and a *small erectile crest*. The *tail is proportionately longer and more graduated* than that of Whitebreasted Cormorant. Imm. is brownish-grey with white underparts. Often seen perched with wings outstretched on a prominent post over water. Occurs on large river systems and in freshwater habitats.

Darter 80 cm

Adult   Immature

B RYAN   P PICKFORD

Resembles a cormorant but has a *thin, almost snake-like head and neck, and a long, stiletto-shaped bill*. The sides of the head and neck are rufous and the mantle and wing coverts are streaked with buff. When swimming, the body is held submerged with only the neck and head showing; the neck is held curved and moves backwards and forwards as the bird swims. Imm. has a white head which darkens with age. Found on dams and rivers.

13

Grey Heron 100 cm

Adult   Immature

A large, long-legged grey bird, often seen standing motion-less in water while fishing. Closer inspection reveals a *yellow, dagger-shaped bill and a white head with black eye-stripe which ends in a wispy crest.* Imm. lacks black eye-stripe and crest, and is duller in colour. In flight can be distinguished from Blackheaded Heron by having a uniform grey underwing. Mostly sol-itary except when breeding. It flies with the head and neck tucked tightly into the shoulders. Occurs widely in salt- and freshwater habitats.

Blackheaded Heron 96 cm

Adult   Immature

The *black top of the head and hind neck contrast with the white throat* and render this heron unmistakable. Imm. has the black on the head and neck replaced with grey and could be confused with imm. Grey Heron but, like the ad., it has *con-trasting black and white underwings*. Not normally associated with water, preferring to forage over grasslands; is attracted to burnt veld.

14

Little Egret 65 cm

A WEAVING

A small white 'heron' with a *black bill and diagnostic yellow toes*. Habitually frequents shallows in freshwater and estuary areas where it feeds by dashing to and fro, repeatedly stabbing at its prey. During this frenzied feeding activity the yellow toes can often easily be seen. In breeding plumage shows wispy white head plumes and lace-like aigrettes on the lower back. Occurs in most freshwater habitats, at coastal estuaries, and at intertidal pools on rocky coasts.

Cattle Egret 54 cm

Breeding   Non-breeding

H VON HORSTEN   G CUBITT

The white 'heron' seen following cattle or game. The breeding bird has a buffy crown, breast and back, and reddish legs; the non-breeding and imm. birds are white, with brownish or greenish legs. Smaller than other white 'herons', and the most gregarious away from breeding colonies, often forming *flocks which follow cattle. They fly to their roosts in tight 'V' formations*.

Hamerkop 56 cm

The *hammer-shaped profile of this bird's head* and bill render it unmistakable. It is a brownish bird with long legs, a large black bill and a shaggy crest. The tail is finely barred. In flight, the bird might be mistaken for a bird of prey were it not for *its long bill and the legs projecting beyond the tail.* Normally associated with water where it wades in the shallows, searching for frogs, but it also patrols roadways in the morning, looking for amphibian road kills.

White Stork 102 cm

A large, *white, heron-like bird with contrasting black flight feathers and a bright red bill.* Legs are also bright red but become covered in excrement and appear greyish-white. Imm. similar to ad. except its bill and legs are duller red and the white plumage is dusted with brown. Congregates to feed, sometimes in large flocks; is particularly fond of lucerne. On hot days is often seen riding thermals in the company of vultures.

Abdim's Stork 76 cm

A WILSON

A black and white stork, considerably smaller than the White Stork with which it often associates. Distinguished from all other similar storks by its diagnostic *white lower back*. At close range, the blue face and greyish legs with red joints are noticeable. Often occurs in very large flocks in agricultural lands. Migrant; more abundant in some years than in others.

Marabou Stork 150 cm

ROY JOHANNESSON

This huge bird is virtually confined to game reserves, where it is seen either soaring over the bush or scavenging at a kill with vultures. The *enormous bill, unfeathered head and neck, and naked, pink fleshy pouch* render this bird unmistakable. Its wingspan approaches that of the Wandering Albatross, the world's longest at almost 2 m. When threatened or displaying, it clappers its large bill.

Sacred Ibis 90 cm

L. VON HÖRSTEN

A predominantly *white bird with a black head and neck* which at close range can be seen to be unfeathered. In flight a *narrow black border to the trailing edge of the wings is visible*. During the breeding season it shows a stripe of bare scarlet skin on the leading edge of the underwing. Imm. resembles ad. but has the head and neck feathered white. Occurs singly or in small flocks near marshy areas and along the western Cape coast.

Hadeda Ibis 76 cm

A WILSON

A dull, *greyish-brown bird with long legs and a long, decurved bill*. At close range an iridescent *bronze patch is conspicuous on the shoulder* and the faint dark and pale lines that run under the eye can be seen. The bill is dark brown but has an almost translucent red ridge. In flight it gives its *distinctive 'ha-ha,ha-ha, de-da'* call from which it derives its name. It is mainly a woodland ibis but forages in glades and grasslands.

African Spoonbill 90 cm

G CUBITT

From a distance, it looks like a white, egret-type bird but when seen at close range, the *long, flattened, spoon-shaped grey and red bill* is diagnostic. The legs, feet and face are bright red. Unlike egrets and herons, it flies with the neck outstretched, and the silhouette of the spoon-shaped bill can be seen. Imm. is generally duller and has dark-tipped flight feathers. When feeding, the African Spoonbill scythes its spatulate bill from side to side through the water. Occurs on freshwater lakes and estuaries.

Spurwinged Goose 100 cm

W R TARBOTON

Readily distinguished by its *large size, black and white pied plumage, and pinkish legs and bill*. The male has a fleshy pink knob on the forehead. Female and imm. are dull brown and have less white in the plumage. Out of the breeding season the birds gather in large flocks on open stretches of water and moult their flight feathers, which renders them flightless for several weeks. Gives a most ungoose-like whistle in flight. Found in freshwater habitats surrounded by grassland and agricultural lands.

Greater Flamingo 130 cm

Adult

Immature

Larger and paler than the Lesser Flamingo: when seen feeding together, this species almost dwarfs the Lesser Flamingo. As a general rule, the Greater is much whiter, having the pink confined to the wings. The *pink bill with a black tip* is diagnostic. Imm. told from imm. Lesser Flamingo by being much larger and having a more massive bill. The call is a goose-like honking. Frequents shallow freshwater lakes, salt pans and estuaries.

Lesser Flamingo 100 cm

Adult

Immature

Much smaller than Greater Flamingo and almost always much redder than that species. Imm. and some pale adults have pale plumage but their smaller size and the diagnostic *deep red bill, which at a distance looks black* should rule out confusion. The Lesser and Greater flamingoes feed in the same manner: with the head submerged upside down as they filter food through the trough-like bill. Both species flock, sometimes gathering in their thousands. The Lesser Flamingo occurs at shallow freshwater lakes, salt pans and estuaries.

20

Egyptian Goose 70 cm

A. WEAVING

 The *chestnut eye patch, white forewings and dark patch on the breast* are diagnostic of this small goose. When not breeding, it occurs in fairly large flocks in open fields or on dams, or on sand bars in rivers. In flocks they tend to be noisy and aggressive birds, attacking each other and giving their loud honking and hissing noises. In flight they form tight flocks in a 'V' formation. Found in freshwater habitats, coastal estuaries and open fields.

Whitefaced Duck 48 cm

W. R. TARBOTON

The *white face (sometimes stained), chestnut breast and barred flanks* help identify this duck. The stance is also characteristic: the body is held very upright and the neck is stretched to its length. The call is a three-part whistle 'wee-wee-weeoo' and is often heard at night when flocks move from one feeding ground to another. Found in coastal lagoons and at shallow edges of lakes, but spends much time ashore.

Yellowbilled Duck 54 cm

N. BRICKELL

The rich, almost *chrome-yellow bill*, which has a black, wedge-shaped patch on top, is diagnostic of this *mottled brown* duck. When the wings are unfolded in flight they show at the base a brilliant blue and green patch (the speculum) which is bordered with black and white. The female gives the characteristic 'quack quack' call, whereas the male has a raspy, hissing call. Found on open stretches of freshwater.

Cape Teal 46 cm

N. BRICKELL

Smaller than Yellowbilled Duck and easily identified by its *mottled greyish plumage and slightly upturned pink bill*. In flight the wing pattern shows two broad white stripes bordering a small green speculum. Differs from Redbilled Teal by lacking the dark cap of that species. The call is a high-pitched nasal whistle which is mostly given in flight. More common in the drier areas of the region, particularly on saline lagoons and lakes.

Redbilled Teal 48 cm

N BRICKELL

This medium-sized brown and buff mottled duck is easily recognized by its *creamy cheeks which contrast with a dark cap and reddish bill*. In flight it shows a buff speculum. The female's call is a soft 'quack'. Out of the breeding season, this duck gathers in substantial flocks, sometimes with other species, on large stretches of open fresh water.

Cape Shoveler 53 cm

N BRICKELL

Distinguished from Yellowbilled Duck by its *black bill* which is spatulate and appears longer than the head. Other features which identify it are the *bright orange legs* and the *powder blue forewings* which are very conspicuous in flight. The female is duller than the male, has a darker head and a smaller patch of blue on the forewings. Occurs in small groups on fresh water, often in company with Yellowbilled Ducks.

Southern Pochard 50 cm

Male

This bird sits low in the water and, on take-off, runs across the water before gaining flight. Rather than upend for its food, this bird habitually dives. The male is distinguished by its *dark plumage*, the *blue bill and bright red eye*. The female is brown with a pale patch at the base of the bill and a *pale crescentic mark on the sides of the face*. In flight both sexes show a

Female

pale belly and have a broad white stripe running down the centre of the wing. Occurs on lakes, dams and vleis; prefers deeper water.

Secretarybird 140 cm

Might be mistaken for a stork or crane when seen striding through the veld but the *short, hooked bill, the black, partly feathered legs and the black, wispy nape plumes* should rule out confusion. In flight it is almost vulture-like except that the *central tail feathers are elongated and project well beyond the end of the tail, as do the long legs.* Most frequently seen in pairs, hunting over open veld, stopping frequently to pick something from the ground or to stamp on some living creature.

ROY JOHANNESSON

ROY JOHANNESSON

N. MYBURGH

Whitebacked Vulture 95 cm

J J BROOKS

The common vulture of bushveld game reserves. If seen when the bird is banking in flight or holding its wings outstretched, the *white lower back contrasts with the darker wings* (diagnostic). Imm. is very much darker than ad. and shows less contrast between flight feathers and wing linings. Most often seen in flight, either riding thermals or high in the air searching the ground for kills. In the early mornings or during cold or overcast, rainy weather, groups can be seen loafing in tree tops. Occurs in open savanna parkland and bushveld.

Yellowbilled Kite 56 cm

A WILSON

The kite seen patrolling roads and frequenting towns and cities. In ad. plumage the *yellow bill and cere* are diagnostic. This large bird of prey is readily distinguished from others by its *forked tail* which it twists in flight from the horizontal to the almost vertical as it steers and manoeuvres through the air. Imm. is darker and has a black, not yellow bill. Call is a whinnying 'kleeeuw' trill. This is the kite commonly seen around human habitation.

Blackshouldered Kite 33 cm

A small, conspicuous bird of prey which is commonly seen sitting on telephone wires and poles, or hovering over the veld or road verges. The ad. is *grey and white with a diagnostic black shoulder patch* and deep, *cherry-red eye*. When perched it occasionally flicks its short white tail. When stooping for food, its wings are held over its back like a parachute. The imm. is dowdier than the ad. and has a buff and brown barred back. It frequents a wide range of habitats from mountains to the coast, and over bushveld and agricultural lands.

H. VON HORSTEN

Blackbreasted Snake Eagle 63-68 cm

A. WILSON

In flight this medium-sized raptor can be easily identified as its *white body and underwings, with primaries and secondaries barred black, contrast sharply with the dark brown head and upper breast*. When perched the dark breast, the proportionately very large, rounded dark head with golden-yellow eyes, and the unfeathered yellow legs are evident. Imm. is a rufous version of the ad. Flight action is light and soaring with the bird frequently hovering. Occurs in thornveld, avoiding open grasslands and forests.

26

Bateleur 55-70 cm

Male

Immature

Female in flight

An easily identified eagle because of its unusual shape in flight: it appears to have *virtually no tail* and has *very contrasting black and white underwings*. The wing shape is also unusual, being narrow at the body and tips and broadening towards the centre. The male has a much broader black trailing edge to the wing than the female. Imm. is a brown version of ad. Flight is direct on slightly canted wings and bird careens from side to side. Found over open thornveld in the major game reserves.

Female

27

African Fish Eagle 63-73 cm

Easily identified by the combination of white head and breast, dark body, chestnut forewings and white tail. Imm. is difficult to distinguish from other brown eagles but it shows a relatively short tail and a shadow image of the adult's white breast. The cry of this bird, a series of gull-like yelps, is very well known in Africa. Always associated with water: coastal lagoons, estuaries, rivers and lakes, but never with the open sea.

N. MYBURGH

P. PICKFORD

Longcrested Eagle 52-58 cm

P. PICKFORD

This small, dark brown eagle is instantly recognizable by its *long, wispy crest* and *white-feathered legs*. In flight it shows distinct white 'windows' in the wings and its barred black and white tail. When not soaring, the flight action is swift and direct with shallow wing beats. In natural forests and exotic plantations these birds may be seen perched on dead trees or telephone poles. The call is a loud, piercing 'wee-aah-wee-aah'.

Steppe Buzzard 45-50 cm

W. R. TARBOTON

Not readily distinguishable from the many similar raptors in the region but most individuals show a pale, broad crescent across the breast. Colours range from almost pale buff to dark brown or black, but the breast pattern is fairly constant. Present only during the summer and then very common, being the most abundant medium-sized raptor seen perched on telephone poles. Flight is strong and direct except when soaring or gliding. Found in open country; avoids deserts and well-wooded regions.

Jackal Buzzard 45-53 cm

B. RYAN

Larger than Steppe Buzzard and not as variable in plumage coloration. When perched appears very dark above, with a bright chestnut breast and barred black and white belly. In flight, the combination of contrasting black and white underwings and bright chestnut breast and tail is diagnostic. Imm. has rufous brown underparts and a comparatively pale tail. Frequents mountainous areas, where it regularly 'hangs' in the strong winds and updrafts.

29

African Goshawk 36-39 cm

Above: adult
Right: immature

A combination of *blue-grey head and dark back* with *pale underparts finely barred with reddish*, helps distinguish ad. Male is smaller than female and brighter. Imm. has reddish barring on underparts replaced with large, drop-shaped dark brown spots, and shows a dark line down the white throat. Seen most often during *early morning display* when it *flies high* over its territory, giving a *short 'whit' call every few seconds*. Occurs in thick evergreen forest, riverine forests in drier areas and exotic plantations.

Gabar Goshawk 30-34 cm

Adult   Immature

Superficially resembles the African Goshawk but has a *grey throat and breast, red, not yellow eyes, cere and legs and a white, not dark rump*. Imm. differs markedly, having a rufous-streaked and mottled head and breast, but it still shows a white rump. A very bold and conspicuous goshawk which regularly sits on exposed perches. An uncommon black form occurs which can be identified by its red cere and legs. Occurs in thornveld and open broadleafed woodland.

30

Pale Chanting Goshawk 54-63 cm

P.R.B. STEYN

Much larger than either the African or Gabar Goshawk and has proportionately *longer legs*. Habitually rests on exposed perches from which it hunts. When put to flight, its *upperparts show a white rump and white trailing edges to the wings and secondaries* which contrast with the darker primaries. Imm. is dark brown above and streaked and blotched with brown below. Name derives from the chanting call given during the breeding season, a piping 'kleeu-kleeu-klu-klu-klu'. Found in the drier western regions and in semi-desert.

Lanner Falcon 40-45 cm

B. RYAN

Above: adult
Below: immature

A medium-sized falcon, the ad. of which shows a *rufous crown and an unmarked pinkish breast.* The imm. has a *buffy streaked crown and heavily streaked underparts.* In flight, this species shows wings which are relatively broad at the base, and which narrow into points. The flight is slow and floppy compared to that of smaller falcons; however, it is rapid when chasing prey and they sometimes execute fast-angled

P. PICKFORD

stoops to strike prey in mid-air. Occurs in a wide range of habitats, from mountains and deserts to open grasslands.

31

Eastern Redfooted Falcon 30 cm

Male

Female

A small falcon whose overall *dark grey plumage* is relieved only by *contrasting white wing linings and a chestnut vent*. The cere, legs and feet are bright red, a feature which can be seen at close range. The female has a pale greyish head with black moustachial stripes, grey upperparts, pale underparts heavily streaked with black, a chestnut vent, and red legs and feet. The imm. is similar to the female but has finer streaking below and has orange, not red legs and feet. Flocks frequent open grasslands, and congregate in trees to roost.

Rock Kestrel 33-39 cm

Male

Very similar to Lesser Kestrel but male has a spotted, not uniform chestnut back, and *lacks blue on his secondaries*. Female very difficult to distinguish from female Lesser Kestrel but Lesser has tendency to form flocks which this species does not. Imm. lacks blue-grey on the head and tail. When hunting it hovers into the wind, remaining stationary with only its wings moving and tail spread before dropping swiftly on to its prey. Rarely seen away from mountainous terrain.

Female

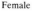

Immature

Lesser Kestrel 30 cm

Male   Female

  Only slightly smaller than Rock Kestrel. The male is distinguished from the Rock Kestrel by having a *uniform chestnut back, and a blue band across the secondaries* of the upperwing. The white toenails are diagnostic but these are apparent only at close range. Female and imm. closely resemble the female and imm. Rock Kestrel but, in summer, the Lesser Kestrel tends to form *large flocks* to feed and roost. Flocks often perch on telephone wires from where they swoop over grasslands to catch insects.

Crested Francolin 33-35 cm

A small, rotund gamebird with a *dark cap that contrasts with a broad white eyebrow stripe.* The upperparts are reddish-brown streaked with buff, and the underparts show a dark freckled neck, throat and breast. Imm. is similar to ad. but has a buff eyebrow stripe. The *tail is often held cocked*, bantam-like, at an angle of 45°. Call is a clear, ringing 'chee-chakla, chee-chakla', given near roosts. Found among heavy tangled growth and along dry river courses in thornveld.

33

Cape Francolin 42 cm

J J BROOKS

This large gamebird is the francolin most frequently seen in fynbos in the southern Cape. At a distance it appears a *uniform greyish-brown with a dark cap* but at close range it can be seen that the plumage is finely vermiculated with grey and buff. Sexes are similar and the imm. is browner than the ad. Occurs in pairs or small groups and is reluctant to take flight, preferring to run off and hide in undergrowth. Call is a loud, rattling 'cacalak-cacalak'. Occurs in fynbos and wheatfields.

Swainson's Francolin 38 cm

P PICKFORD

This large brown francolin is easily distinguished by having *bare red skin around the eyes and on the throat* and this, combined with its *dark brown legs* is diagnostic. Sexes are similar and the imm. is a dowdier version of the ad. At dusk and dawn the male gives a 'krraae-krraae-krraae' crow from an elevated perch. Occurs in small groups and frequents a variety of habitats, mainly dry thornveld and agricultural lands.

34

Helmeted Guineafowl 56 cm

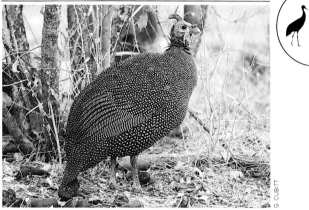

A familiar bird, easily distinguishable by its rotund body and greyish plumage finely spotted with white. The *naked blue and red head has a red crown casque and wattles*. Large groups sometimes form and the birds run around excitedly, chasing one another. When put to flight, they burst from cover and fly clumsily in follow-my-leader style before alighting some distance off. Occurs in grasslands, broadleafed woodland, and thornveld; has become domesticated on farms.

Crowned Crane 105 cm

Adult

This large, long-legged bird is unmistakable. When in flight, the *large white wing patches are conspicuous*. Imm. lacks the bold white face patches of the ad. and has a less well-developed bristly golden crown. Has a diagnostic *honking call in flight*. Birds form large flocks when not breeding. Displaying birds dance around facing each other, holding their wings outstretched. Frequents marshes, dams and adjoining grasslands.

Blue Crane 100 cm

RAYMONDE JOHANNESSON

The national bird of South Africa. Overall impression is of a *large, long-legged, greyish bird with a paler head and long drooping tail.* However, the actual tail is very short and the drooping feathers are elongations of inner wing feathers. Feathers on the breast are also elongated and sometimes give the bird a shaggy-breasted appearance. This bird performs a dancing display with the wings outstretched. Associated with freshwater areas and open grass-lands but has adapted to agricultural lands.

Black Crake 20 cm

H VON HÖRSTEN

A small, furtive bird with matt black coloration, a *yellow bill and red eyes and legs*. Imm. is a greyish-brown version of the ad. and has a dark bill and dull red legs. A noisy bird, more often heard than seen. More inclined to venture from cover into the open at dawn and dusk, when it may be seen darting over floating vegetation. Will also climb reed stems and can be seen clambering up and clinging to reed stalks. Occurs in marshes and swamps with a thick cover of reeds.

Purple Gallinule 46 cm

A WILSON

This large, reed-dwelling bird has a bright purplish-blue head and underparts, and a green back offset by bright white undertail coverts. The *large bill and frontal shield are bright red*, as are the legs and long toes. When creeping about in reedbeds it flicks its tail up and down, revealing the white undertail coverts. It regularly ventures into open areas adjoining thick cover. In flight the legs and toes project well beyond the tail, giving a heron-like outline. Frequents flooded grasslands and thick reedbeds.

Moorhen 32 cm

N MYBURGH

Much smaller than Purple Gallinule which it resembles in that it has a red frontal shield, but this species has a *yellow tip to the bill* and has green, not red legs and toes. Plumage is sooty black but there is a diagnostic *white stripe on flanks*, and the outer undertail coverts are white. Swims with jerky movements and constant flicking of tail, on open water. Imm. is greyish-brown version of ad. Occurs in freshwater areas surrounded by a thick cover of reeds and grass.

Redknobbed Coot 44 cm

ROY JOHANNESSON

Above: adult
Below: immature

W.G. McILLERON

A medium-sized, matt *black, duck-like bird with an ivory-white bill and unfeathered forehead.* The two red knobs situated on the top of the white shield are more conspicuous during the breeding season but are only noticeable at close range. Imm. is similar to imm. Moorhen but is larger and more grey in appearance, and lacks the white undertail coverts. Sometimes found in large flocks; dives regularly to feed. Likely to occur on any stretch of fresh water, except fast-flowing rivers.

Kori Bustard 135 cm

H. VON HORSTEN

This is the heaviest bird in the world and is by far the *largest bustard of the region:* its size alone should rule out confusion. The female is noticeably smaller when compared to the male. It is usually seen striding across the open veld, swinging its head and neck with a peculiar backwards and forwards movement. Reluctant to fly unless directly threatened. When displaying, the male gives a deep-throated booming and fluffs out the large white feathered areas on his neck. Found in dry thornveld, open grasslands and semi-desert.

38

Black Korhaan 52 cm

Male

Female

This small korhaan is unmistakable, especially when the male is seen in flight display during the breeding season. The male, a striking black, white and barred brown bird, flies into the air and courses over its territory, calling continually. At the end of the display it slowly descends to the ground with slow-motion wing beats and with its bright yellow legs dangling. The female is drabber and has the black restricted to the lower belly. Inhabits dry coastal scrub, open grassland and thinly wooded thornveld.

African Jacana 28 cm

Adult

Immature

A rufous bird with a darker belly, white throat and breast and yellow foreneck. The *black and white head pattern which offsets a blue frontal shield and bill* is diagnostic. The *toes and toenails, which are exceptionally elongated* to allow walking on floating vegetation, are conspicuous. Imm. is duller, with a paler head and underparts. On landing, this species often holds its wings open over its back. Occurs in flooded grasslands and freshwater areas that have floating vegetation.

39

African Black Oystercatcher 40 cm

A WEAVING

A medium-sized *black wader which has an obvious orange-red bill*, dull pink legs and a bright orange ring around the eye. Imm. is dowdier and has a less vividly coloured bill. When in flight, the bird appears all black and has no wing markings, although a few individuals may show some white on the underparts. Usually found in pairs but larger groups form between breeding seasons. Found along rocky coasts and on sandy beaches.

Whitefronted Plover 18 cm

A WEAVING

A small, pale plover likely to be confused with imm. Kittlitz's Plover but this species generally has a paler breast, a much *paler, sandier coloured back and a black marking on the forehead.* Imm. lacks dark marking on head and is paler than ad., with buff edging to feathers of the back and mantle. Frequents sandy beaches, muddy coastal areas and large river systems.

Kittlitz's Plover 16 cm

J J BROOKS

Above: adult
Below: immature

 This small plover is distinguished by its cinnamon-coloured underparts and by the *black line on the forehead which extends behind the eye on to the nape*. Imm. lacks the black head markings of ad. but is darker than similar Whitefronted Plover and has a dark shoulder mark. Not often seen on open beaches, it occurs in small flocks sometimes far from water; prefers short grassy areas and dried muddy patches.

A. WILSON

Threebanded Plover 18 cm

W R TARBOTON

This small plover has an overall elongated appearance and frequently bobs its head and tail. The *double black breast band* is diagnostic; this species also shows a *grey face and throat*, red eye ring and red base to the bill. Although it occurs singly or in pairs on smaller stretches of water, at certain times of the year large numbers may gather at favoured freshwater dams.

Grey Plover 30 cm

A. WILSON

A medium-sized wading bird which is drab grey, lightly speckled with white above, and off-white to white below. The head is relatively large and the bill is short and black. Only in flight are the diagnostic *black armpits* clearly visible. In breeding plumage (rarely seen in the region) the underparts are jet black and the upperparts are spangled with silver. When feeding, these birds remain motionless and then dart forward to pick up their prey. Found on open estuaries, bays and lagoons.

Crowned Plover 30 cm

W.R. TARBOTON

A very familiar wader not associated with water but commonly encountered in towns and villages where it frequents grassy road verges and open sportsfields. Readily identified by its brownish plumage with a white belly and the diagnostic *black cap surrounded by a white 'halo'*. The bird's legs are bright vermilion, as is the bill base. Very active and noisy at night when the raucous 'kreeep' call can be heard.

Blacksmith Plover 30 cm

H. VON HORSTEN

This large *black, white and grey bird* is the easiest plover to identify and the bold wing pattern makes it readily distinguishable in flight. The imm. is a duller version of ad. with brown feathering replacing the black. When alarmed and put to flight, the bird gives a rapid, *metallic 'tink tink'* call and, if the breeding territory is invaded, it will dive-bomb the intruder. Found near damp areas at wetland edges and adjoining grasslands.

Turnstone 23 cm

A. WILSON

This small wader can be seen running over pebbly beaches or poking about in strands of rotting seaweed. Its *bill is short, slightly flattened and upturned* and with this it busily *overturns small stones* or prods aside seaweed in search of food. The upperparts are dark and the pale underparts show irregular dark markings on the front and sides of the breast. The legs are relatively short and are *bright orange with darker joints*. In flight it shows *heavily patterned wings and tail*.

Common Sandpiper 19 cm

A WILSON

This small, usually solitary wader has a peculiar habit of *bobbing backwards and forwards* between short bursts of running. It is uniformly drab brown above and white below, with the *white on the breast curving up and over the shoulder*. In flight the wings are held slightly *bowed downwards and are flicked rapidly between short glides*. Flight call is a characteristic 'tee tee tee'. It occurs in a wide range of wetland habitats.

Wood Sandpiper 20 cm

A WILSON

Has a bobbing action similar to that of Common Sandpiper but not as exaggerated. Identification points are the *brownish back, well spotted with buff or white, the white rump and barred tail* (best seen in flight), a pale grey underwing, and long greenish-yellow legs which project well beyond the tail in flight. When alarmed and in flight gives a shrill 'chif if if' call. Spotting on upperparts appears much reduced when plumage is worn. Occurs on dams, vleis, bays and estuaries.

Curlew Sandpiper 19 cm

A small wading bird with longish legs and a *long decurved bill*. Appears very grey in the field; in flight shows a *broad white rump* and a noticeable wing bar. Breeding plumage is totally different: rufous underparts and brightly patterned upperparts, but the whitish rump is still evident. Feeds by walking belly-deep in water and probing its bill into mud. Found in a wide variety of wetland habitats, but is most common in coastal estuaries.

Greenshank 32 cm

A medium-sized, very pale grey wader which has a *slightly upturned, dark-tipped grey bill* and long, *greyish-olive legs*. In flight it shows a *conspicuous white rump which extends up the back in a white wedge*. It is often seen running around in the shallows chasing small fish. It gives a ringing 'chew-chew-chew' in flight and when startled. Frequents a wide range of fresh- and salt-water wetlands.

Bartailed Godwit 38 cm

L. HES

This large wader is easily recognized by its *very long, up-turned bill, the basal half of which is pink*. The non-breeding bird is mottled grey and brown above and white below, but in breeding plumage the underparts assume a rich orange-brown colour. In flight it shows a *white rump and finely barred tail, and dark upperwings*. Frequents estuaries, bays and muddy-edged lakes where it freely wades out into deep water to feed. Sometimes gathers in large groups to roost.

Whimbrel 43 cm

A. WILSON

From a distance, might be confused with the Bartailed Godwit but this bird has a *long decurved bill*. At closer range, the diagnostic *black stripes on the head*, bisected by a pale stripe down the centre of the crown, and the pale eye-stripe can be seen. In flight it shows a *conspicuous white rump which extends on to the lower back*. Invariably gives a staccato whistled call note when flushed. Found in estuaries, coastal lagoons and bays.

Avocet 42 cm

W.R. TARBOTON

An unmistakable, large black and white wader with a *long, very thin upturned bill*. The legs are long and blue and the feet are partly webbed. In flight the *three black patches in each wing* make a very striking pattern. Frequents lakes and vleis where the birds regularly swim, dipping their heads and bills under water. Gives a sharp, rattling call in flight. Occurs in pairs when breeding but forms large flocks at other times.

Blackwinged Stilt 38 cm

W.R. TARBOTON

This wader is distinguished by the combination of its exceptionally *long pink legs* and its *black and white plumage*. The bill is long, black, very thin and pointed. Female and imm. have the black on the back and wings tinged with brown; the imm. has extensive brown markings on its hindneck and head. The breeding male shows a black nape and crown. Rarely flocks. Inhabits marshes, vleis, saltpans and flooded areas.

47

Spotted Dikkop 44 cm

J J BROOKS

A *cryptically coloured* wading bird with a large head and big yellow eyes. The bill is short and yellow at its base and the legs are greenish-yellow. Plumage is mottled brown, buff and black and in flight shows two small *white patches in the upperwing*. Occurs away from water and is active at night, resting up during the day under bushes or in other shade. When defending its territory, the wings are held fully spread and slightly forward to display the white wing patches. Found in dry sparse bush and overgrazed areas.

Subantarctic Skua 60 cm

J C SINCLAIR

A *large brown seabird* which resembles an imm. Kelp Gull but lacks the white rump and shows conspicuous *white patches at the base of the primaries*. This bird, the largest member of the skua family, has a heavy body, broad-based wings and mottled brown plumage. Some birds show a tawny head and throat. Flight is normally slow and ponderous but when chasing another seabird to pirate its prey, it thrusts forward on powerful wings. Found over open oceans, rarely venturing inshore.

Kelp Gull 60 cm

L. VON HORSTEN

Above: adult
Below: immature

P. PICKFORD

The largest gull in the region. The ad. is easily identified by its white body, *jet black back and upperwings and bright yellow bill* with an orange spot at the tip. Imm. plumage is very variable but in the first year the bird is very dark brown with a pale rump; it becomes paler with age. Found at estuaries, and at coastal and inshore waters.

Greyheaded Gull 42 cm

W R TARBOTON

Above: adult
Below: immature

A. WEAVING

Differs from Hartlaub's Gull by having a *dove-grey head, pale eye* and bright red bill, legs and feet. It is also slightly larger bodied and has a longer, heavier bill than Hartlaub's. Imm. Greyheaded has more extensive dark markings on the head, paler legs, a pink bill with a dark tip and a more extensive black tip to the tail than imm. Hartlaub's. Although this gull occurs in coastal and freshwater areas, it breeds inland, away from the sea.

49

Hartlaub's Gull 38 cm

L. HES

Slightly smaller than Greyheaded Gull with a *darker red bill and legs*, and dark eyes. In breeding plumage shows a *faint grey hood*, but in non-breeding plumage has a completely white head. Imm. has faint brownish markings on the head, the black tip to the tail is either reduced or absent, and it has a brown, not two-tone bill as in imm. Greyheaded Gull. This is the small gull common along the southern Cape coast.

Caspian Tern 50 cm

A. WEAVING

Non-breeding

The *largest tern* in the world, it is instantly recognizable by its conspicuous *coral-red bill*. In breeding plumage has totally black cap but when not breeding and in imm. plumage has the cap streaked black and white. Imm. has an orange bill and dark-edged back feathers. In flight the shallowly forked tail and the black tips to the underside of the primaries can be seen. Call is loud, harsh 'kraaak'; imm. gives a weak, nasal whistle. Found in the vicinity of large rivers, estuaries, bays, lagoons and inshore waters.

N. MYBURGH

Breeding

Swift Tern 46 cm

Smaller than the Caspian Tern, this species has a *yellow not red bill*. At long range it shows a plain white underwing. In breeding plumage has black cap ending just before the bill, imparting a white forehead; when not breeding has variable amount of black on forehead but appears mostly white or grizzled. Imm. has *mottled upperparts and extensive black on head* but still shows yellow bill. Frequents islands, larger estuaries and bays.

Right: breeding
Below: non-breeding

Common Tern 33 cm

During summer, the most abundant small tern on the southern African coast. Has many features in common with most small, non-breeding terns (grey upperparts, white underparts, and a partially developed black cap). Subtle aids to identification are the long, slightly decurved bill and uniform grey rump. In breeding plumage (attained in March-April), the bird has a wholly black cap, pale grey underparts, a very long forked tail and a bright red, black-tipped bill. Often forms vast roosting flocks on beaches and at river mouths.

Whitewinged Tern 23 cm

The most abundant small freshwater tern in our area. The non-breeding plumage is *pale grey and white* with *small amounts of black on the head and underwing*. In breeding plumage (seldom seen in the region) the bird is a striking contrast of *black, grey and white*, with the *silvery forewings* being most noticeable. Flight can be almost butterfly-like and is very buoyant as the bird dips over water to pick up food. Occurs mostly over freshwater areas but is also found at larger estuaries.

B RYAN

Below: breeding   Above: non-breeding

A WILSON

Namaqua Sandgrouse 25 cm

A pigeon-sized bird and, in the region, the only sandgrouse with a *long pointed tail*. In flight has very rapid wing beats and often gives its nasal 'kalke-ven' call which reveals its presence. The male has a buff-spotted back and a white and chestnut breast band; the female is cryptically mottled and streaked with buff and brown but still shows the pointed tail. Inhabits dry grasslands, and true and semi-deserts.

N MYBURGH

Above: female
Below: male

N MYBURGH

Feral Pigeon 33 cm

P. PICKFORD

This is the *common street pigeon* familiar to anyone who lives in a city. It occurs in a variety of plumages: the most common colour combination is a dark grey body, an iridescent sheen on the neck, a white rump and pale grey wings which show two black bars. Away from cities, it is often seen in the vicinity of farmsteads or in flocks of racing pigeons winging across the veld.

Rock Pigeon 33 cm

L. VON HORSTEN

Appears very dark in the field but, at close range, the finely *white-speckled reddish back* and wings and the *bare red skin around the eyes* are diagnostic. Occurs in flocks, and is sometimes found in substantial numbers over stubble cornfields; has adapted to urban life and is frequently seen on ledges of buildings. Call is very owl-like, with a deep resonant 'hoo-hoo' and it echoes through the cliff caves and ledges this species frequents in nature.

Rameron Pigeon 42 cm

By far the *largest dove or pigeon* in the region and appears the darkest of all. Only in bright sunlight or at close range can the *bright yellow bill, bare skin around the eyes and on the legs and feet be seen*. The plumage is a mixture of dark maroons, grey and blue, finely speckled with white. In flight the bird appears almost black but the sun often highlights the yellow bill or feet. Found in evergreen forests and exotic plantations.

Redeyed Dove 35 cm

The largest and darkest of the 'ring-neck' doves. The eye and the bare skin surrounding it are red – a feature normally seen only at close range. Unlike the Cape Turtle Dove it shows *no white in the tail* but it does have a *grey band on the undertail* and a diagnostic *black band at the base of the tail*. Imm. is very similar to ad. but has a reduced ring on the neck. Ranges from dry bushveld to coastal forests; has adapted to towns and cities.

Cape Turtle Dove 28 cm

The 'ring-neck' dove which shows a diagnostic *white tip and sides to the tail in flight*. This dove is much paler and *smaller than the Redeyed Dove* which lacks white in the tail. Probably the most abundant dove in the region, its three-note call is a familiar background sound in the veld. Display flight consists of the bird flying up at low angle and then descending slowly with wings and tail spread. It occurs in a wide range of habitats; avoids coastal forest.

Laughing Dove 26 cm

Smaller than the Cape Turtle Dove and *lacks the black hind collar* of that species. It has a *pinkish-grey body, pale blue forewings and a finely black-speckled breast*. In flight lacks the white tail tip seen in the Cape Turtle Dove but has conspicuous white outertail feathers. The call, from which it derives its name, is a chortled cooing. Not present in arid areas but inhabits a wide range of bush and farmlands and occurs in many towns and cities.

Namaqua Dove 28 cm

Male

A small-bodied dove which has a *long pointed tail, and a black face and throat.* In flight the combination of the long pointed tail, pale underparts and chestnut flight feathers render this bird unmistakable. Shows iridescent blue spots on the wings. The imm. and female lack the black face of the male but show a shorter pointed tail and chestnut flight feathers. Prefers drier regions such as thornveld, scrub and semi-desert.

Female

Greenspotted Dove 22 cm

A small dove which is often seen in game reserves when it is flushed from roadsides or congregates at waterholes. In flight it shows *reddish wing patches* and *two black bars on its rump*; it is only at close range and in sunlight that the *green wing spots* can be seen. The characteristic call is a series of descending 'du-du' notes. Found in thornveld and dry, broadleafed woodland.

Brownheaded Parrot 24 cm

A. WILSON

A small, *brown-headed parrot which at rest appears very green* and is difficult to see in a leafy canopy; often it is the bird's screeches and squawks that indicate its presence. In flight, which is very rapid, the *bright yellow underwings* are visible. Imm. is a duller version of ad. Frequents thornveld, riverine forest and open woodland.

Knysna Lourie 46 cm

ROY JOHANNESSON

A large *green bird with a long tail and crest*. Distinguished from the Purplecrested Lourie by greenish plumage, white-tipped crest and whitish marks above and below the eye. Groups frequent tree canopies where they run along the larger branches, raising and lowering their tails. In flight, they show *brilliant red patches on the wing tips*. The call is a loud, far-carrying 'kow kow kow'. Occurs in dense evergreen forests.

Purplecrested Lourie 46 cm

A WILSON

Superficially resembles the Knysna Lourie but is very much *darker*. It has a *dark purple crest which appears black* unless seen in good light, it lacks the white markings and crest tips of the Knysna Lourie and has bare red skin around the eyes. It behaves very much like the Knysna Lourie in that it keeps to tree tops where it leaps nimbly from branch to branch, showing the bright red wing patches. Found in evergreen, coastal and riverine forests.

Grey Lourie 48 cm

A large, uniformly *grey bird with a long tail and crest*, it is often seen in groups perched on the top of thorn trees, where it looks like a giant mousebird. Flight is strong, with flapping alternating with gliding. Members of a group fly in single file, in follow-my-leader fashion. The call is a diagnostic 'go-away' or variations of this; when calling, the bird raises its crest and flicks its tail. Frequents thornveld and dry woodland.

ROY JOHANNESSON

Whitebacked Mousebird 34 cm

H. VON HORSTEN

Most likely to be confused with the Speckled Mousebird from which it is best differentiated at rest by having *red legs and feet and a pale bill tipped with black*. In flight the *back shows a white stripe narrowly bordered with black* and this is diagnostic. It behaves in much the same manner as the Speckled Mousebird but is more agile and has a more powerful flight. Inhabits thornveld, fynbos scrub and arid regions.

Speckled Mousebird 35 cm

N. MYBURGH

A small, drab, *long-tailed bird* which occurs in small groups and creeps about in bushes, mouse-like, and hangs from branches. When flushed, the birds fly to the next bush in 'follow-my-leader' fashion and virtually crash-land. Distinguishable from the White-backed and Redfaced Mouse-birds by its *black face, black and white bill, and brown legs*. Occurs in thick tangled bush, and fruiting trees in suburban gardens.

Redfaced Mousebird 34 cm

A WEAVING

Easily distinguished from other mousebirds by being pale *greyish in colour* and by having the *bill base and the naked skin around the eye bright red*. Flight action is very different from that of other mousebirds in that it is direct, fast and powerful with the birds flying in small groups or in single file. The call is a diagnostic three- or four-note whistled 'whee-whe-whe'. Found in thornveld, open broadleafed woodland and suburban gardens; avoids dense forest and desert.

Redchested Cuckoo 30 cm

W G McILLERON

This cuckoo's *three-note call 'weet-weet-weeeoo'* is diagnostic and is often the only indication of the bird's presence as it is extremely difficult to discern in the leafy canopy it frequents. It is normally only seen as it swiftly departs, when the very *dark back and chestnut breast* instantly identify it. Imm. is very dark above and is heavily barred black below. A bird of evergreen forest and exotic plantations.

Black Cuckoo 30 cm

J.C. SINCLAIR

More often heard than seen but is fairly obvious when glimpsed in the canopy or when foraging lower down in a tree. It might be confused with its host, the Forktailed Drongo, but lacks the forked tail. It differs from the black morph Jacobin Cuckoo by *lacking the crest and white wing patches*. The call is a mournful, droning 'whooo-wheeee', repeated frequently. Inhabits woodland and forests, exotic plantations and suburban gardens.

Jacobin Cuckoo 34 cm

E.P. HELM

An all-black morph occurs which might be mistaken for a Black Cuckoo but this species shows a diagnostic *wispy crest and white patches* at the base of the primaries. Pale phase birds are black and white with a long tail, crested head, white wing patches and lack any striping on the underparts. It is most often detected by its 'klee-kleeu' call. This species occurs in woodlands, preferring thornveld.

Diederik Cuckoo 18 cm

Adult   Immature

During summer the 'dee-dee-dee-deederic' call is a familiar sound in and around the weaver and bishop colonies that these birds parasitize. When not calling they can be distinguished from the similar Klaas's Cuckoo by their more contrasting bottle-green and white plumage, more extensive white behind the eye, and white flashes on the wings and shoulders. At close range the bright cherry-coloured eye can be seen. This species occurs in open grasslands with stands of trees, in thornveld and exotic plantations.

Burchell's Coucal 44 cm

Most often seen sitting on an exposed perch either drying itself after a downpour or sunning itself in the early morning. It is a large bird and is easily identified by its *black cap, chestnut back and wings* and *long black floppy tail*. Some birds have a white-flecked head with a broad white eyebrow stripe. The call, usually given before or after rain, is a liquid, bubbling series of notes. Normally shy and furtive, this species occurs in long grass, riverine scrub and reedbeds.

Spotted Eagle Owl 43-50 cm

P PICKFORD

The most frequently seen *large owl with 'ear' tufts*. It is normally a *greyish-brown mottled and barred* bird but it may be *richer brown in colour*. This owl has adapted to suburbia where it is a regular sight on driveways or roofs and its hooting call may be heard in the evenings. If disturbed at its daytime roost in a thickly foliaged tree, it holds its large yellow eyes partially closed. Frequents a variety of habitats, but avoids dense forest.

Barn Owl 34 cm

P.R.B STEYN

Active at dusk or dawn, this owl appears very pale and is totally silent on the wing. At rest during the day, the *white, heart-shaped face with black eyes*, and faintly spotted, light buffy underparts with richer golden upperparts identify this owl. When startled during the day, it moves from side to side while peering at the intruder. Found near human habitation but will roost in caves, mineshafts and hollow trees.

African Scops Owl 20 cm

The call of this *diminutive owl* is an often-heard 'night noise' in the bushveld and it is usually taken to be a frog. When seen in torchlight, the *tiny size, greyish 'bark-like' plumage and long ear tufts* identify this bird. When roosting during the day, it compresses its body, huddles against a tree trunk and slits its eyes, making it almost impossible to detect. Occurs in bushveld and dry open woodland.

Fierynecked Nightjar 24 cm

Nightjars are nocturnal and are very difficult to observe; even if flushed during the day, identification depends on a few seconds' view before the bird vanishes. The features to look for in the male are the white markings on the tail and wings, and in the female the *white outertail spots* which differentiate it from similar nightjars. The bird's call, which is given at night, is a diagnostic, whistled 'whuee-whe-whe-whe-whe-whe' with the last notes rapidly descending in pitch. Found at the edge of woodland, in bushveld and exotic plantations.

Malachite Kingfisher 14 cm

L. VON HORSTEN

Usually seen fleetingly as it passes low over the water. When fishing, remains motionless for long periods, perched on a reed stem or branch overhanging water, and is often overlooked. The crown is *barred black and turquoise*, the back is an *iridescent blue* with a *turquoise rump*, and the *underparts are reddish-brown and white*. The bill in the ad. is bright red and is a useful identification feature, but the imm. has a blackish bill. Frequents reedbeds surrounding lakes, lagoons, streams and rivers.

Woodland Kingfisher 23 cm

W. R. TARBOTON

Much more brightly coloured than the Brownhooded Kingfisher and has a *black lower mandible and red upper mandible*, not an all-red bill. Differs further from the Brownhooded Kingfisher by having a *blue head, back and tail*. A common bushveld bird, it is often seen perched on a tree top displaying with outstretched wings and giving its sharp, piercing 'trrp-trrrrrrrr' call. The imm. is dowdier and its black lower mandible shows some red patches. Inhabits thornveld, broadleafed woodland and riverine forest.

Brownhooded Kingfisher 24 cm

P. PICKFORD

A much *duller bird than other red-billed kingfishers*. Easily identified by its *all-red bill, brownish, streaked head*, chestnut patches on the sides of the breast, and streaked flanks. Shows less blue on wings and lower back than the Woodland Kingfisher, but this is still very evident in flight. Sits motionless on perch waiting for prey and in a blue flash will descend rapidly to the ground to snatch an insect or lizard. Occurs in thornveld, open broadleafed woodland and coastal forests; has adapted to suburban gardens.

Pied Kingfisher 28 cm

SABI SABI

Male

The only kingfisher to have a *pied black and white plumage*. The bill is exceptionally long. The male has a double black breast band whereas the female has only a single. Before plunging for its fish prey, this species either perches on a branch overhanging water or it hovers and then dives. It sometimes occurs in small groups whose members interact excitedly, giving a twittering call and a high-pitched 'chik-chik'. Found on any stretch of open water, coastal lagoons and rock pools.

66

Striped Kingfisher 18 cm

A WEAVING

A small, dull bushveld kingfisher which is easily recognized by its dark-capped appearance which contrasts with a pale collar, the fine streaking on its breast, and a red and black bill. The call is a high-pitched 'cheer-cherrrrr' and, when calling in display, it will raise its wings to show the black and white patterned underwing and blue back. The latter is more obvious in flight. It frequents thornveld, and riverine and coastal forests.

Narina Trogon 34 cm

L HES

Male

Frequents the canopy and mid-storey of forests and is never easy to see. Although it is very brightly coloured, the bird habitually sits with its green back to the observer and is thus well camouflaged in its leafy surroundings. A front view will reveal the *bright red breast and belly with a whitish undertail*. The female lacks the green throat of the male, has a duller crimson breast and is generally dowdier. It occurs in riverine and evergreen forests and dense, broadleafed woodland.

European Bee-eater 28 cm

In flight this bird shows a *dazzling array of colours* with its *chestnut to golden back contrasting with turquoise-blue underparts* and almost translucent rufous wings. At rest the bright yellow throat bordered by a narrow black gorget can be seen. The imm. has a greenish back and pale blue underparts. Groups fly high, uttering the characteristic, far-carrying peawhistle-like 'prrrup' call. Frequents thornveld, broadleafed woodland and adjacent grassy areas.

H VON HORSTEN

Little Bee-eater 17 cm

N MYBURGH

The smallest bee-eater and probably the most widespread and common. Easily identified by its *small size, green back and buffy underparts, yellow throat with black gorget,* and square or slightly forked tail which lacks projections. Always seen in pairs or small groups hunting insects from low perches. The russet underwings are conspicuous when the bird dashes out to catch insects. Frequents edges in thornveld and clearings in coastal forests.

Whitefronted Bee-eater 24 cm

In flight appears very *green with a dark blue undertail* but at rest the *red and white throat and white forehead* are diagnostic. Has a square-ended tail and lacks pointed tail projections. Hunts insects from a perch, sallying forth to take prey in flight, and then returns to the same perch. Nest colonies, which are sometimes large, are situated in steep sandy cliffs cut by wide, slow-moving rivers. The birds are active and noisy around the nests, giving nasal 'qrrruk-qrrruk' calls.

A. WEAVING

European Roller 31 cm

W R TARBOTON

Superficially resembles the Lilacbreasted Roller but *lacks the long outertail feathers* of that species and has a *clear blue breast* and has much more *chestnut on the back*. In flight it appears paler than the Lilacbreasted Roller and has a *square-ended tail*. Although the imm. Lilacbreasted Roller has a square-ended tail, it has a lilac-washed breast. Catches insects on the wing or by swooping from a perch to the ground. Found in thornveld and open grasslands with scattered trees.

Lilacbreasted Roller 36 cm

This species is commonly seen in some game reserves. It frequently perches on telephone poles and wires, from where it swoops to catch its insect prey. In flight it shows a range of pale and dark blues in the wing. At rest, the lilac breast and long, pointed outertail feathers are diagnostic. When displaying, the male will perform a complex flight in which he rolls from side to side on the downward stoop. Occurs in mixed areas of thornveld, broadleafed woodland and along roadsides.

Hoopoe 28 cm

The combination of a *pinkish-brown body* and striking *black and white wings and tail* is diagnostic. The *black- and white-tipped crest* is often held closed but the bird will raise it if alarmed or on alighting. When feeding it walks with a jerky gait and probes its long bill into the ground, searching for insects. The call is a soft 'hoop-hoop-hoop'. Inhabits thornveld, broadleafed woodland, and parks and gardens.

Redbilled Woodhoopoe 36 cm

The ad. is a large, *glossy blue and green bird* with a *long, graduated, white-tipped tail* and a *long, red, decurved bill* and red feet. The imm. is not as glossy as the ad. and has a black, not red bill. Small groups clamber through foliage and up tree trunks, using their bills to probe for insects. The cackling call is some-times given by the whole group; birds sway backwards and forwards while calling. Occurs in woodland and thornveld.

Scimitarbilled Woodhoopoe 26 cm

Likely to be confused only with the imm. Redbilled Wood-hoopoe which has a black bill but this species is *smaller and its bill is much thinner and more decurved*. In flight the white patches in the wings and the long, graduated, white-tipped tail can be seen. It appears black at a distance but, in direct sunlight, the glossy purple and blue plumage is evident. Frequents thornveld and dry, broadleafed woodland.

Trumpeter Hornbill 58-65 cm

A WILSON

Male

This large black and white hornbill is instantly recognizable by its *black bill and large casque*, and its *red face*. The female and imm. have smaller casques, pied plumage similar to that of the male, and reddish faces. The species has a dipping flight action, with noisy wing flapping interspersed with glides. The call is a diagnostic wailing, resembling the sound of a baby crying. Found in evergreen, coastal and riverine forests.

Grey Hornbill 46 cm

W R TARBOTON

P PICKFORD

Male   Female

The *only small hornbill that has a dark bill*. The female might be mistaken for a Southern Yellowbilled Hornbill because the top of her bill is creamy yellow but she has a dark head and breast, and a conspicuous white eyebrow stripe. The imm. is very similar to the female. Flight action is very floppy and buoyant. The call is a series of piping notes. Occurs in thornveld and broadleafed woodland in drier areas.

Redbilled Hornbill 36 cm

Plumage resembles the Southern Yellowbilled Hornbill's but this species has a *shorter, more slender red bill*. Distinguished from all other hornbills with red bills by its *small size*. Imm. has a duller, less well-developed bill and has buff, not white spotting on the wings. Display consists of the bird bobbing its head and giving a 'kokwe-kokwe-kokwe' call with its wings held slightly open. Usually occurs singly or in pairs but may flock when not breeding. Inhabits thornveld and mopane woodland.

Southern Yellowbilled Hornbill 55 cm

Resembles the Redbilled Hornbill but is far larger and has a more *massive yellow, not red bill*. The female Grey Hornbill, which has a creamy yellow top to her bill and might be confused with this species, has a dark head and breast. Feeds mostly on the ground where it hops, not walks; frequents picnic sites in game reserves. Display is similar to that of the Redbilled Hornbill: it spreads its wings while giving its 'tok-tok-tork-tork' call notes. Inhabits thornveld and broadleafed woodland.

73

Ground Hornbill 90 cm

An unmistakable, *turkey-sized* bird with a *long, decurved black bill* and conspicuous *naked red face and throat*, the latter often slightly inflated with air. Imm. differs from ad. by showing yellow, not red face and throat patches. Occurs in small groups or family parties which *walk, on tiptoes,* through the veld. Usually flies only when deliberately flushed and has a cumbersome flight; shows *broad white wing patches.* Call is a loud booming 'oomph oomph' given early in the morning. Occurs in open grassland in thornveld, broadleafed woodland and upland grasslands.

Above right: adult
Right: immature

Blackcollared Barbet 20 cm

Instantly recognizable by the *bright red face and throat broadly bordered with black*. This bulbul-sized bird has a short tail, chunky body and very thick bill. Imm. has the face and throat brown, streaked with red and orange. Pairs duet in display by sitting together and bobbing up and down, giving a ringing 'too-puddly' call. Occurs in thornveld, broadleafed woodland and coastal forest.

74

Pied Barbet 18 cm

N. MYBURGH

Similar in shape to the Blackcollared Barbet but is smaller and has diagnostic *black and white plumage, a red forehead and yellow spotting on the back* and wings. Might be confused with the Redfronted Tinker Barbet but is much larger, has a black bib and a more massive bill. Mostly solitary or in pairs and gives a nasal 'nehh-nehh' or a Hoopoe-like 'doo-doo-doo' call. Found in dry broadleafed woodland, thornveld and arid scrub.

Redfronted Tinker Barbet 11 cm

W. G. McILLERON

This small barbet might be confused with the larger Pied Barbet but has a white throat and much more yellow streaking on the upperparts. Very similar to the Yellowfronted Tinker Barbet but has a *red, not yellow forehead* and generally has brighter yellow streaking above. Usually solitary but may gather in small numbers at fruiting trees. Occurs in moist broadleafed woodland and forest.

Yellowfronted Tinker Barbet 11 cm

B RYAN

Very similar to the Redfronted Tinker Barbet, but their ranges do not overlap so there is little chance of confusion. The yellow on the forehead is not readily discernible on this tiny barbet and the overall appearance is that of a greyish streaked bird with a yellow wash on the wings and pale underparts. When seen, the yellow forehead can sometimes appear a rich orange colour but it never attains the bright red of the Redfronted Tinker Barbet. The call is a continual and monotonous 'konk konk konk' metallic sound and is repeated rapidly.

Crested Barbet 23 cm

N. MYBURGH

The largest of the barbets, this species is unmistakable with its orange-yellow face, *black shaggy crest and broad black breast band*, white and golden speckled back, and crimson rump. Much more terrestrial than other barbets, it hops around with an upright stance, but when it does fly, the flight is rapid and direct. The song is a diagnostic trilling which has been likened to the ringing of a muffled alarm clock. Occurs in open broadleafed woodland, thornveld and riverine forest; has adapted to suburban gardens.

Lesser Honeyguide 15 cm

W G McILLERON

This small and unobtrusive bird can easily be detected by its distinctive call – a far-carrying 'klew klew klew' – which is given from the same perch and is repeated regularly. It is overall dull greyish, with a greenish wash on the wing coverts, a small dark moustachial stripe and conspicuous white outertail feathers. It is often seen being harassed by barbets and, as it dashes through the canopy, its white tail feathers are conspicuous.

Goldentailed Woodpecker 23 cm

The loud, nasal 'whee-eeeeaa' shriek and bill tapping on wood often reveal the presence of this bird. When it is seen clinging to a tree, the best identification features to look for are the *streaked underparts, buff and yellow spots on the olive back*, and the *black and red crown* and *red moustachial stripe*. It climbs vertical tree trunks with jerky movements, using its tail as a brace. Found in thornveld, open broadleafed woodland and coastal forests.

W R TARBOTON

Right: male

Cardinal Woodpecker 15 cm

Very much smaller than the Goldentailed Woodpecker and is the *smallest woodpecker* in the region. Sometimes difficult to locate when feeding in thick bush or leafy canopy but its incessant tapping on a branch often reveals its position. Paler and less streaked below than the Goldentailed Woodpecker, it has a *buff and yellow barred, not spotted back*. Flight action is fast and undulating. Frequents a wide range of habitats from thornveld to thick forests.

N. MYBURGH

Left: male

Rufousnaped Lark 18 cm

B RYAN

Most often seen during the breeding season when it perches on small bushes or termite mounds singing a simple 'tree-lee-treelooe' phrase. Often flicks its wings during song phrase. It less regularly gives a display flight during which the song becomes a jumbled chattering. Best recognized by its calls, combined with a *rufous nape* and *large rufous wing patches* which are conspicuous when the bird flushes. Found in open grasslands with stunted bushes, thornveld and agricultural lands.

Spikeheeled Lark 15 cm

J SOBEY

This small lark has an upright stance on long legs, and a long, slightly decurved bill. Its remarkably *short tail is black underneath and has a contrasting white tip* that is very noticeable in flight. The plumage varies from region to region but in general the bird shows *buffish underparts which contrast with a white throat*. It usually occurs in small groups. Found in grassland, scrub desert and desert gravel plains.

Sabota Lark 15 cm

L HES

A small, nondescript lark which has no obvious display flight or diagnostic song. Its habit of sitting on small trees and telephone wires and delivering its jumbled song full of mimicry are pointers to its identification. It has a short, thick bill, a buff or white eyebrow stripe which imparts a capped appearance, and it lacks the rufous wing patches seen in many other similar species. Frequents thornveld, open broadleafed woodland and scrub.

Redcapped Lark 16 cm

N. MYBURGH

A conspicuous and sometimes very common lark which gathers in flocks outside the breeding season. Colour can vary from area to area but the combination of a *red cap and red shoulder smudges* are diagnostic. The underparts are *white to off-white* and *clear*, unlike those of any other lark in the region. The call given by flocks in flight is a sparrow-like 'tchweerp'. Found in a wide range of habitats from desert to moist grasslands.

Greybacked Finchlark 13 cm

N. MYBURGH

Above: male
Below: female

N. MYBURGH

This small grey and black bird is often flushed from road verges in the drier regions, especially the Karoo. When seen on the ground the diagnostic coloration of *totally black underparts, greyish upperparts* and *black and white patterned head* are clearly visible. The female is small and squat like the male, also has a pale conical bill and greyish upperparts, but has only a patch of black down the centre of the belly. Occurs mostly in small flocks when not breeding. Ranges from cultivated lands to scrub and true deserts.

European Swallow 18 cm

W R TARBOTON

Probably the most common swallow in the region between the months of November and March; before migrating in March large numbers are often seen *resting on telephone wires*. They roost in dense reedbeds, sometimes in hundreds of thousands. The ad. has a *brick red face and throat, a blue-black breast band* and off-white to buffish underparts. The tail streamers are very long and there are white spots on the tail base. Occurs over virtually any habitat; roosts in reedbeds.

Greater Striped Swallow 20 cm

W R TARBOTON

Likely to be confused only with the Lesser Striped Swallow from which it is distinguished by being much *larger*, and by being far *paler* in overall appearance, with *faint striping* on white underparts discernible only at close range. The crown is pale orange and the *pale rufous on the rump* does not extend on to the vent. A common roadside bird in many areas especially near culverts, which it uses for breeding sites.

Lesser Striped Swallow 16 cm

Noticeably *smaller* than the Greater Striped Swallow, it differs in plumage by being *very heavily streaked on the underparts* and by having a *rich rufous rump* which extends on to the vent. It also has a much richer rufous cap and nape. It occurs at lower altitudes than the Greater Striped Swallow and is frequently found in the vicinity of buildings, on which it builds its nest.

South African Cliff Swallow 15 cm

Might be confused with the Greater and the Lesser Striped Swallows but this bird has only a *slightly notched tail*, is *more rufous below* with much *reduced streaking*, and has a *distinct breast band*. Has adapted to nesting under road bridges and similar man-made structures and is commonly seen along the roadside or perched on wire fences.

82

Rock Martin 15 cm

L VON HORSTEN

A medium-sized martin and the only one with all-brown plumage. It could be confused with the dark form of the Brownthroated Martin, but that species is smaller and shows a white belly and vent. The Rock Martin has the underparts slightly paler than the upperparts and, in flight, white spots are visible on the spread tail. It prefers rocky and mountainous terrain but has adapted to towns and cities, where it nests freely on buildings.

Redbreasted Swallow 24 cm

J VAN JAARSVELD

This obviously *very large swallow* is readily identified by its conspicuous *rufous underparts* (diagnostic). In flight it can be seen that the red on the breast extends to the wing linings and forms a collar over the nape. The remainder of the plumage is a dark glossy blue and may appear black in some lights. It is usually encountered in pairs along roadsides or in mixed flocks of swallows. Found over open grassland in thornveld, and broadleafed woodland and upland grassland.

Whitethroated Swallow 17 cm

ROY JOHANNESSON

The gleaming *white throat contrasts with the black breast band and greyish underparts*. A small red patch on the forehead is visible at close range. The remainder of the plumage is a glossy blue-black, and white spots are visible in the centre of the tail when the bird banks in flight. It is usually seen in pairs, generally near water, nesting under bridges and road culverts.

Black Cuckooshrike 22 cm

J.L. VILJOEN

W.G. McILLERON

Male   Female

The male is an *all-black*, slightly glossy bird with an *inconspicuous yellow gape* and a more obvious *yellow shoulder* although the latter feature is not always present. The female is very different, *resembling a female cuckoo* with her *green and yellow barred plumage*, but is larger and has bright yellow outertail feathers. Unlike flycatchers and drongos, this bird creeps through foliage, gleaning insects from the undersides of leaves. Frequents a variety of woodlands, from coastal forest to bushveld.

Forktailed Drongo 25 cm

A *conspicuous and noisy bird* which often perches freely in the open from where it hawks insects in flight or drops to the ground to retrieve food. It has a *deeply forked tail* and appears black all over, but in flight the underwing primaries can reflect light and the wing then appears pale edged. Fearless of large birds of prey, it frequently chases buzzards and even eagles, dive-bombing them from great heights. Inhabits a wide range of woodland, forest and open areas.

L. HES

Blackheaded Oriole 24 cm

W. P. STANFORD

A bright, *golden-yellow bird* which has a *black head and throat, black wings* patched with white and a bright coral-red bill. The female is similar to the male; the imm. differs by having a brownish head streaked with yellow and a dull red bill. Although very brightly coloured, it remains well concealed in the leafy canopy and is difficult to detect unless its fluty song or the harsher 'kweeer' note is heard. Found in a mixed range of woodlands, bushveld and exotic plantations.

Black Crow 50 cm

B. RYAN

The only *all-black crow* likely to be seen in the veld, far from human habitation. The bill, which is slightly de-curved, is longer and *more pointed* than that of any other crow. At close range it can be seen that the plumage coloration ranges from oily black to glossy deep blues and purples. Pairs are usually seen sitting aloft some man-made structure, calling to each other and flicking their wings. Occurs in upland grasslands, open country, cultivated fields and arid regions.

House Crow 42 cm

J.C. SINCLAIR

A common and ever-increasing bird in the Durban region where it occurs in close association with the larger Pied Crow. Easily identified by its long thin body and tail, *dark grey body and black face, wings and tail*. A general scavenger in suburbia in coastal cities, occurring in small flocks but forming large roosts in trees in the evenings.

86

Pied Crow 50 cm

Unmistakable: the only crow in the region to have a *white belly*. Could possibly be confused with the Whitenecked Raven when seen in flight at long range but this species has a longer tail and a smaller, more compact head. Seldom seen in flocks unless attending a kill in a game reserve or roosting in trees near cities. Regular visitor to rubbish dumps.

Whitenecked Raven 54 cm

When seen at close range, the *massive black bill with a white tip and the white crescent on the nape* are diagnostic. In flight it is distinguished from other crows by its shape: large, heavy head, broad wings and a *short, broad tail*. Very aerodynamic, they often ride air currents in mountainous terrain, twisting and diving or chasing one another. The call is a very deep and throaty 'kwook'. Inhabits mountainous regions, open country and upland grasslands.

87

Southern Black Tit 16 cm

A typical tit in both behaviour and calls: its harsh chirring notes are often the first indication that a bird feeding party is in progress. The male and female are similar but the male is *more black*, less grey than the female and has a large area of *white in the wings* and white-tipped undertail coverts. Found in evergreen and coastal forest and thornveld.

H VON HORSTEN

Left: male

Ashy Tit 13 cm

N MYBURGH

This small bird has a *slate grey body*, white-fringed wings, a *black cap, white cheeks, and a black throat and bib* extending as a black line down the belly. Very active; continually on the move through thickets, pecking and probing for food and regularly hanging upside down. Occasionally feeds on the ground where it hops about with a very upright stance. It travels in pairs or small parties, keeping in contact with a variety of ringing calls. Occurs in thornveld, broadleafed woodland and riverine scrub.

Arrowmarked Babbler 24 cm

A very familiar bird in many parts of the region. This species habitually travels in groups, with members of the flock following one another, either feeding on the ground or flying up to trees. The birds keep up a constant soft chatter; however, if something alarms them, the *chatter builds into a crescendo.* Larger than a bulbul, this babbler appears generally drab brown but at close range the *arrow-like white markings* down the throat and breast and the *pale eye* are visible. Occurs in thornveld, broadleafed woodland and exotic plantations.

L. VON HORSTEN

Blackeyed Bulbul 22 cm

H. VON HORSTEN

Probably one of the most familiar birds in most parts of the region as it has adapted successfully to cities and towns and commonly frequents gardens. It does not have a black eye as its name suggests but does have a soft, unfeathered *black wattle around each eye.* This distinguishes it from the Redeyed Bulbul which has a red wattle. The more obvious features shared by these bulbuls are the *black head* and *bright yellow undertail coverts.* Occurs in thornveld, evergreen forests and is common in gardens.

89

Cape Bulbul 21 cm

N. MYBURGH

Unlikely to be mistaken for the Blackeyed or Redeyed Bulbul as the ranges do not overlap, and this species is easily identified by its *conspicuous white eye wattle*. It is also a much darker bird, having the dark head colour extending well on to the breast and belly. Is less confiding and not as habituated to man as other bulbuls. Inhabits fynbos, coastal scrub, riverine forests and exotic plantations.

Redeyed Bulbul 21 cm

J.J. BROOKS

Easily distinguished from the Cape and Blackeyed Bulbuls by its diagnostic *red eye wattles*. Other less obvious differences are a *darker head* and an overall *slightly paler appearance*. The ranges of these three bulbuls rarely overlap; this species is found in the more arid regions where it is a common bird around waterholes. Its call is a liquid 'cheloop chreeep choop' and a shorter 'kwit-kwit' alarm note. An inhabitant of river courses in dry thornveld and scrub areas.

90

Kurrichane Thrush 22 cm

N. BRICKELL

Often shy in its natural environment, this bird has adapted to parks and gardens in many areas and become bold, venturing out on to open lawns in search of food. When disturbed it will fly up into a tree and sit motionless until the intruder has passed. It closely resembles the Olive Thrush but has a *bright orange bill* and a speckled white throat with obvious *black moustachial stripes*. Alarm call is a distinct 'peet-peeooo'. Frequents thornveld, open woodland and parks and gardens.

Olive Thrush 24 cm

N. MYBURGH

In many respects the Olive Thrush is very similar to the Kurrichane Thrush but it has a *yellow bill*, a *dusky speckled throat* and lacks the black moustachial stripes. Forages in leaf litter but it will also take berries and fruit. Early in the morning it gives a rich, melodic song which is a variation on a whistled 'wheet-tooo-weet' phrase. Occurs in evergreen forests, coastal scrub, and parks and gardens.

Cape Rock Thrush 21 cm

A fairly shy and unobtrusive bird of rocky hillsides, it sometimes ventures into picnic sites where it becomes bold, picking up food scraps. The male is easily identified by his *entirely blue head* which contrasts with the *orange breast*. The female is duller, being a rusty red on the head and body. The male often perches on a rock or boulder, with the bill pointing skywards, and gives his soft whistled song. Frequents mountainous and rocky terrain, both at the coast and inland.

Above: male
Above right: female

Groundscraper Thrush 22 cm

Much bolder than other thrushes and is frequently seen hopping around in parks and gardens and at picnic sites in game reserves. When foraging on the ground it often raises a wing, as if saluting, revealing a *contrasting black and white pattern on the underwing*. Has a very upright stance and this, combined with the *bold facial markings* and the *heavily spotted breast*, makes identification easy. The song is a clearly whistled phrase. Found in dry thornveld, open broadleafed woodland, and parks and gardens.

Mountain Chat 20 cm

Above: male
Right: female

When driving over mountain passes or through rocky arid areas, the startling black and white bird which flushes from the roadside is most likely to be this species. Very flighty and nervous, it will not allow close approach but the very obvious *black and white pied plumage* should render it unmistakable. It could be confused with the male Stonechat but the latter is much smaller and has a rufous breast. Some males are greyish instead of black but all show a *white cap, shoulder patch and rump*. The female is greyish and nondescript but also shows the diagnostic white rump. Inhabits mountainous and rocky terrain.

Capped Wheatear 18 cm

A bird of the open level veld with little grass cover and plenty of termite mounds to use as look-out posts. It has a very upright posture at rest. It can run very rapidly and, when it flies, its *white rump and sides of the tail* are conspicuous. The *white eyebrow stripe, black cap and black collar* are diagnostic. In display, the male hovers over the female and his territory and gives his jumbled warbling song. Found in barren sandy or stony areas and in short grasslands.

Familiar Chat 15 cm

A WEAVING

A small, dark greyish-brown bird which lacks any obvious field characters except its behaviour. Most small chats have the habit of nervously *flicking their wings* slightly open, which exposes the rump and uppertail which are normally boldly patterned: the Familiar Chat continually performs this *wing-flicking motion*, and displays a *russet rump and outertail feathers*. It inhabits rocky and mountainous terrain, and open woodland in some areas.

Anteating Chat 18 cm

D BUTCHART

Associated with the open veld and termite mounds on which it perches with an upright posture to scan its territory. Always occurs in pairs or small parties and is very active, taking short flights, hopping across the veld or *hovering into the wind* before darting off downwind. Appears black but at close range its rich *chocolate-brown plumage* can be seen. Some males have a *white shoulder patch* but all birds show white 'windows' in the wing tips, a feature visible only in flight.

Stonechat 14 cm

A small chat, the male of which has conspicuous plumage of a *black head, bright white sides to the neck, a rufous chest, white patches in the wings and a white rump*, all of which are very obvious in flight. The female is far drabber, lacking the black head and having rusty brown plumage but she also shows a white rump. Almost always occurs in pairs and is common in many areas; has adapted to the canefields of Natal. The call, a 'weeet' followed by a harsh 'chaaak', sounds like two stones being tapped together, hence its name. Inhabits upland grasslands, open treeless areas with short scrub, and sugarcane plantations.

N MYBURGH

L VON HÖRSTEN

Above right: male
Right: female

Natal Robin 18 cm

N BRICKELL

This small forest robin is extremely shy and furtive, preferring to keep to the darker tangles of thickets in evergreen forests where, during the day, it forages in leaf litter. At dusk and dawn it becomes more confiding and will enter open areas at the forest edge to feed. The bright *orange-red plumage with powder-blue wings* is diagnostic. The normal call is a frequently repeated 'see-saw' note.

Cape Robin 18 cm

N. MYBURGH

This shy robin is easily recognized by its *short white eye-brow stripe and by having the orange coloration confined to the throat and upper breast*. It feeds mostly on the ground but creeps up through vegetation and sits on an exposed perch to sing. Imm. is mottled and spotted buff but shows a *reddish tail with a dark centre*. Song is a short warbled phrase and the alarm call is a harsh 'grrrr'. Frequents montane river valley scrub, evergreen forests and fynbos.

Whitebrowed Robin 15 cm

A. WILSON

A bird which is heard more often than seen, as it sings from deep within a bush. The song is very variable but the usual phrase is a short 'tchweet-chereee-wheeet'. The bird has diagnostic *heavy streaking down the breast, a white eyebrow stripe, and white spots in the wing* which form a white wing bar. The tail tip is spotted white; the tail is frequently raised and lowered, displaying the russet rump. Found in both dry and moist broadleafed woodland, thornveld and forest.

Heuglin's Robin 20 cm

An explosive rush of melodious and repetitive song from thick, tangled scrub early in the morning often indicates the presence of this species. It is furtive but, if seen, the *red-orange underparts*, and dark head with a *broad white eyebrow stripe* soon identify the bird. The imm. is drabber than the ad. and has buff-tipped feathers on the mantle and back. Occurs in dense riverine thickets and tangles, and parks and gardens.

Karoo Robin 17 cm

This small greyish bird is common in the fynbos of the south and west and in the more arid regions. It is easily recognized if flushed as the *black tail*, which is held *fanned in flight, shows a conspicuous white tip*. The overall plumage is *drab grey, slightly paler below, and there is a short white eyebrow stripe* and a russet base to the tail. It feeds on the ground, hopping about with its tail cocked; it dashes for cover when disturbed. It perches on small shrubs to deliver the short, jumbled song. Frequents semi-arid scrub and fynbos.

97

Titbabbler 15 cm

Most often seen as it creeps through thick thorn bush delivering its loud, explosive song. It is a *greyish bird with a longish tail*, *chestnut vent* (diagnostic), and a pale eye. The folded wing shows a *chequered shoulder* and the *throat is streaked black*. The song is rendered as a liquid 'cheruuup-chee-chee', interspersed with harsher chattering notes. Occurs mostly in pairs which maintain contact through their fluty calls. Inhabits dry thornveld, thickets and dry scrub in arid regions.

Cape Reed Warbler 17 cm

A confusing variety of small birds frequents thick stands of reeds and this warbler is one of them. It is relatively common and is present throughout the year. It appears much like any other drab warbler but is *fairly large* and has *brownish upperparts and clearer white underparts* than similar warblers. Often seen low down on the edge of reedbeds, flitting among the stems, collecting insects from the water's surface. Its *liquid, melodious song* is characteristic of reedbeds. Frequents reedbeds adjoining wetlands.

African Sedge Warbler 17 cm

N MYBURGH

Dark brown with a long tail, if glimpsed this bird resembles a rodent as it scuttles close to the base of reed stems. When displaying during the breeding season the male gives a series of fast 'brrrup' call notes and performs a short *fluttery flight among the reeds or just above them*. During the flight the *short rounded wings* and *long heavy tail* are noticeable. It also gives a cat-like mewing call. Inhabits reedbeds adjoining dams, lagoons and large rivers.

Barthroated Apalis 13 cm

J J BROOKS

This *small, long-tailed bird* is easily identified by its *greyish or greenish upperparts, creamy underparts with a thin, dark bar across the breast* and a pale, creamy eye. It might be mistaken for the Yellowbreasted Apalis but lacks any yellow on the breast. Occurs in pairs in forest or scrub and creeps through the mid-stratum or low down, gleaning insects or caterpillars from under leaves. The song is a rapidly repeated 'pillip-pillip'. Frequents ever-green and coastal forests, scrub and fynbos.

Yellowbreasted Apalis 13 cm

W.P. STANFORD

Male

Apalises are lively, *long-tailed warblers*, continually on the move in forest or bush and, although many of them remain high in the canopy, this species prefers the lower or mid-stratum. It can be identified by the combination of a *greyish cap, white throat and bright yellow breast* which, in the male, has a *small black bar* on the lower breast. The call is a fast, buzzy 'chizzek-chizzek' which is repeated frequently. Occurs in thornveld and broadleafed woodland.

Longbilled Crombec 12 cm

N. MYBURGH

A small greyish bird with *buffy cinnamon underparts, this species appears almost tailless*. It is easily distinguished from similar warblers as the bill is long and noticeably decurved. This active bird occurs in pairs or small groups and is a regular attendant at bird parties. It feeds by gleaning insects from branches and leaves and will probe crevices with its long bill. The call is a frequently repeated 'tree-trriit'. Occurs in a wide range of woodlands and semi-arid scrub; avoids moist forests.

Bleating Warbler 12 cm

N MYBURGH

This species resembles the well-known Wren of the northern hemisphere. It keeps low down in thick vegetation and habitually *cocks its tail*. It has *off-white to greyish underparts and olive-green upperparts*; the race found in the more arid regions has a grey, not olive back. When excited or disturbed, it will flit through the undergrowth giving a metallic clicking sound but the normal call is a loud, snapping 'bidup-bidup-bidup'. Found in moist evergreen forests, dry broadleafed woodland and thornveld.

Fantailed Cisticola 10 cm

N MYBURGH

Cisticolas are notoriously difficult to identify and the Fantailed is no exception unless the bird is calling or displaying. It is a tiny bird with a finely streaked forehead and well-marked buff and black back. The tail, which is short and often held fanned, has a dark subterminal band and a white tip. In its display flight, the bird *flies around* at no great height in a bounding, erratic manner, *continually giving its 'zit-zit-zit-zit' call*. It occurs in grasslands, preferring damp or marshy areas.

Greybacked Cisticola 13 cm

N. MYBURGH

This, the common cisticola in fynbos and arid Karoo scrub, is *long-tailed* and has a *grey-streaked back and chestnut cap.* For most of the year it is unobtrusive and skulks in scrub but when breeding it becomes obvious with its aerial display and calls. The call, a loud, muffled 'prrrttt' followed by sharp 'phweee-phweee-phweee' notes, is given in a fluttery low flight over its territory. It is found in fynbos, grassy hillsides and desert scrub.

Rattling Cisticola 13 cm

B C. HARMSE

The most abundant cisticola of the thornveld and probably the most conspicuous of all the cisticolas. It perches openly on the tops of bushes and proclaims its territory with a *loud 'chureee-chureee'* song, that ends with a *rattling 'cherrrrr'.* When one is walking through the bush, this is the small, long-tailed bird with a *chestnut cap* which approaches and boldly scolds with a consistent 'cheee-cheee' alarm note. Frequents thornveld, broad-leafed woodland and the edge of coastal forest.

Spotted Prinia 14 cm

P. PICKFORD

The common prinia found in low scrub and bracken and briar habitat in the fynbos, Karoo and some mountainous areas. Unlikely to be confused with other prinias or cisticolas because of the *diagnostic streaking on its breast*. Like other prinias, it has a long tail which is often held cocked at right angles. An easily agitated bird often seen perched on a grass stem giving its sharp 'chleet-chleet-chleet' call.

Marico Flycatcher 18 cm

L. VON HÖRSTEN

A nondescript flycatcher which has *uniform dun brown upperparts* and *clear white underparts*. At close range a buffish ring around the eye and a buff panel in the wings are discernible. At rest, the bird appears very *white breasted and has an upright stance*. It uses prominent perches from which it hawks insects; it often returns to the same perch. Occurs in pairs and small groups and is a common roadside bird in mixed thornveld and dry broadleafed woodland in the drier north-western regions.

Fiscal Flycatcher 20 cm

Male   Female

This bird resembles a Fiscal Shrike but it has a *shorter tail* with *obvious white patches on either side, it lacks white on the shoulders* and has a short, fine bill and not the thick, hooked bill of a shrike. Its habits also differ in that it behaves like a flycatcher and does not sit in such exposed situations as the Fiscal Shrike. The imm. is brown, not black. Occurs singly or in pairs and is normally silent. Inhabits fynbos, mountainous scrub and open broadleafed woodland.

Cape Batis 13 cm

A large and chunky batis. The male shows *russet over the wings and flanks* as well as a broad black breast band; the female might be mistaken for the Chinspot Batis but has the *russet breast band extending down the sides of the breast and over the flanks*. It occurs in pairs and in bird parties and is an active flycatcher in the mid-canopy. Found in moist evergreen forest and heavily wooded gorges in mountainous areas.

Chinspot Batis 13 cm

Male

A small black and white flycatcher, the female of which has a *broad chestnut breast band* and a diagnostic *chestnut spot on the chin*. The male lacks the chestnut spot and its *breast band is black*. Normally occurs in pairs. Will glean insects from foliage as well as hawk flies, which it does with an audible snap of the bill. Call note is a clear, whistled 'teuu-teuu-teuu' and harsher 'chrr-chrr-chrr' notes. Occurs in dry broadleafed woodland and thornveld.

Female

Paradise Flycatcher 23 cm, plus 18 cm tail

The male Paradise Flycatcher is unmistakable. It has an *extraordinarily long tail which, like the back, is rufous and contrasts with the blue-grey underparts* and darker head. The female and imm. lack the very long tail. An active and noisy bird, whose harsh 'tic-tic-chaa-chaa' notes are often heard before the bird is seen. Dashes about in the midcanopy chasing insects, rarely settling at one perch for very long. Frequents a wide range of woodland habitats.

Male   Female

African Pied Wagtail 20 cm

A WILSON

Unmistakable and unlikely to be confused with any other species in the region. The *black and white plumage*, combined with the *long tail which is continually bobbed* up and down, is diagnostic. The female has a sootier breast band than the male. Feeds on the ground, usually in damp areas close to water, but may be found far from water. Dashes to and fro chasing insects, its tail busily moving up and down. Call is a 'chee-cherooo'.

Cape Wagtail 20 cm

RAYMONDE JOHANNESSON

A much dowdier bird than the African Pied Wagtail, with the black being replaced by *greyish-brown which sometimes has an olive wash*. Habits very similar to those of the African Pied Wagtail, with much running around and *tail wagging* when chasing insects. Prefers damp and marshy areas but will frequent watered grassy lawns in parks and gardens. When not breeding, large flocks may gather to form communal roosts in trees.

Grassveld Pipit 16 cm

A. WILSON

The pipit most likely to be seen in the open veld or grasslands near towns and cities. It is fairly nondescript: *buff and brown* with *streaking on the breast*, and *prominent white outertail feathers* visible in flight. Always feeds on the ground where it runs short distances, stops to pick up food and then stands with a very upright posture. In display flight the bird flies high in a series of bounding loops, finally plummeting in a spiral with its wings held over its back.

Orangethroated Longclaw 20 cm

A. WEAVING

Most often encountered when flushed in the veld: in flight, the tail is usually held spread, showing the white tips, and the flight is on stiffly held wings which are kept spread below body level. The back is well streaked and mottled. Only on landing, and when the bird is facing the viewer, can the brilliant orange throat, surrounded by a black band and duller orange-yellow underparts, be seen. The call is a cat-like mewing and a loud whistled 'cheeruup'. Occurs in coastal and upland grasslands.

Yellowthroated Longclaw 20 cm

J SOBEY

A long-legged and long-toed bird of grasslands which has a proportionately *short, white-tipped tail* which is conspicuous in flight. The underparts are *bright canary-yellow and there is a broad black gorget*. When flushed, the bird flies with jerky wing beats and glides with its tail spread, showing the white tips. It frequently alights on the top of a bush and utters its loud, whistling 'phooooeeet' call. Found in grasslands adjoining wetlands, coastal lagoons and estuaries.

Fiscal Shrike 23 cm

ROY JOHANNESSON

ROY JOHANNESSON

Superficially resembles the Fiscal Flycatcher but is more robust in build, has a much longer tail and has *white shoulder patches*. It also has a more *powerful bill* which is obviously hooked. The female has a *rufous patch on the flanks* and the imm. is mottled brown above and has grey barring below. A common and familiar bird, which hunts from perches in exposed situations. When perched, it often holds its tail at an angle to the body. Found in a wide range of habitats but avoids dense forests.

Above left: male
Left: female

Redbacked Shrike 17 cm

Male   L. HES   Female   A. WILSON

A small, colourful shrike which has a *grey head and rump, black mask* through the eye, a black tail and very conspicuous *chestnut back and wings*. The female is drab brown above with a pale eye-stripe and fine brown barring on the underparts. A typical shrike, it perches in exposed positions from where it can scan the ground for the insects on which it feeds. It also skulks and, when disturbed, will retire to thickets to hide. Found in broadleafed woodland and thornveld.

Southern Boubou 23 cm

L. VON HORSTEN

ROY JOHANNESSON

Although it resembles a Fiscal Shrike, the Southern Boubou is unlikely to be mistaken for the former species because of its very different habits. It is difficult to see as it keeps well hidden in deep tangles in the undergrowth and rarely ventures into the open. When glimpsed, the impression is of a *black and russet bird with a white wing bar*. The female has slaty grey, not black upperparts, and is more rufous below than the male. The call is often heard as members of a pair keep contact by duetting a 'booo-booo' followed by a 'whee-ooo', and variations on this. It is a bird of dense thickets in riverine and evergreen forests.

Above left: male
Left: female

Crimsonbreasted Shrike 23 cm

Unmistakable: one of the most startlingly coloured birds of the dry bushveld. The brilliant *crimson underparts* contrast with the *jet black upperparts* which are offset by a *white flash down the wing*. Although very brightly coloured, it can be difficult to see as it tends to skulk in the undergrowth. However, it often feeds on the ground and sometimes in fairly open areas. The call is an unusual clonking sound and a harsh 'grrrr'. Found in thornveld and dry river courses.

Puffback 18 cm

Female

This small shrike is a noisy and conspicuous member of bird parties foraging in the mid- and top canopy. The male has a *jet black cap and obvious red eye, a grey and black back* and a diagnostic *white rump*. In display, the male fluffs his rump feathers into a *fur-like white ball* and dashes through the foliage in pursuit of the female. The female is paler than the male. They have a variety of contact calls. Frequents a wide range of woodland and forest.

Blackcrowned Tchagra 23 cm

W.R. TARBOTON

This species is shy and furtive and when flushed from cover will fly quickly to the next bush, briefly showing its *chestnut wings and white-tipped black tail*. Only when the diagnostic *black line down the centre of the crown* is seen can a positive identification be made. It sometimes feeds on the ground but mostly is seen as it moves through the lower tangles of bush. The whistled crescendo of this shrike is a typical bushveld sound. Occurs in mixed thornveld and riverine scrub.

Bokmakierie 23 cm

D. BUTCHART

This robust shrike is a familiar bird in many areas and its call is commonly heard. The ad. is easily recognized by its *grey head, green back and bright yellow underparts with a black gorget*. The imm. lacks the black gorget, but the undertail, like that of the ad., has conspicuous yellow tips which are obvious in flight. Display consists of head bowing and tail raising by both adults as they face each other. Found in fynbos, Karoo scrub and scrub-filled valleys in mountainous areas.

White Helmetshrike 20 cm

D. BUTCHART

Always seen in small groups flitting through open woodland in follow-my-leader style. Flocks are conspicuous when they take flight as they show their *pied black and white plumage with a lot of white in the wings and tail*. At rest the bird shows a *grey crest, white collar*, clear white underparts and a black tail. The *yellow eye wattle* is noticeable at close range. Found in mixed woodlands and thornveld.

European Starling 21 cm

P. PICKFORD

Non-breeding

During the breeding season the ad. is an *iridescent green, blue and black* but appears all black when not seen in sunlight, and the bill is bright yellow. The non-breeding bird is conspicuously spotted with white and has a dark bill, while the imm. is brown and has a paler throat. Sometimes occurs in large flocks, especially when roosting or feeding in fields. Song is a bubbling jumble of squeaks and mimicry. Occurs in cities, towns and farmlands.

Indian Myna 25 cm

P. PICKFORD

A starling-sized bird which, in flight, shows conspicuous *white patches in the wings and a white-tipped tail*. At rest it appears brown with a glossy black head, a *bright yellow bill, bare yellow skin around the eyes,* and yellow legs. A noisy inhabitant of cities and towns where it feeds on open lawns and fields and along roadsides. Gathers in large roosts in the evenings and is generally considered a pest.

Pied Starling 27 cm

L. VON HORSTEN

This large, dark brown, almost black starling is readily identified by its *conspicuous white vent and undertail coverts*. At closer range the pale eye and the *yellow base to the bill* are noticeable. It feeds on the ground, often among livestock, and will search for ectoparasites on animals' backs. Forms large flocks in the early morning and evening, flying at considerable height to and from the roosting areas. The call is a loud 'skeeer-kerrra-kerrra'. Occurs in open grasslands and areas under cultivation.

113

Wattled Starling 21 cm

P PICKFORD

A WEAVING

Breeding male   Non-breeding

In flight appears similar to the imm. European Starling but the Wattled Starling has a *pale rump*. A *greyish bird with black wings and tail*, during the breeding season the male attains wattles and becomes very conspicuous, showing his *black and yellow patterned head*. When breeding, this species forms large colonies which nest in trees and bushes. Has a sharp 'sreeeeo' call note. Found in grasslands, thornveld and broadleafed woodlands.

Plumcoloured Starling 19 cm

R P B ERASMUS

The male of this small starling is an unusual *glossy amethyst colour on the head, throat and upperparts* but, at a distance, it appears black and white. The female is very different: *her drab brown upperparts and heavily streaked underparts* impart a thrush-like appearance. This species is seen in pairs or small groups in trees, rarely on the ground. The call is a short 'tip-tip-tip'. Inhabits moist woodlands and thornveld; avoids evergreen forests.

Above: male
Below: female

A WEAVING

Glossy Starling 25 cm

P. PICKFORD

The iridescent coloration of this bird is evident only in direct sunlight; at a distance, it can appear black. The bright orange eye is wide, staring and button-like. There are two rows of black spots on the wing coverts and the bird can be distinguished from the Blackbellied Starling by its brighter glossy plumage and by having an *iridescent greenish-blue, not black belly*. It occurs in pairs or small parties and does not normally form large flocks. Found in thornveld, mixed woodlands and suburbia.

Blackbellied Starling 21 cm

P. PICKFORD

Resembles the Glossy Starling but is less glossy, with a *matt black belly and flanks*, and has a yellow, not orange eye. It is also noticeably smaller and more slender than the Glossy Starling and has a proportionately longer tail. It frequently forms large flocks out of the breeding season and is much noisier and more demonstrative than the Glossy Starling. Occurs in coastal and riverine forests in the east.

Redwinged Starling 27 cm

A. WILSON

Above: male
Below: female

P. PICKFORD

This *large, long-tailed starling* is easily recognized in flight when the bright *chestnut primaries* can clearly be seen; at rest, the chestnut is not normally visible on the folded wing. The male is a slightly glossy dark blue, while the female is duller, with a dark grey head and breast but she still shows the chestnut primaries. Sometimes occurs in large flocks. Call is a whistled and often mournful 'cherleeeoo' or 'peeyoo'. Inhabits rocky ravines, and cliffs; has adapted to surburbia.

Redbilled Oxpecker 22 cm

L. HES

This species is usually seen peering over the back of a large mammal and giving its scolding 'chrrrr' call note and a hissing 'zzzzzzzist'. As it scrambles over the animal's body looking for ticks, the *large red bill* and the *bare yellow skin around the eye* are clearly visible. Young birds have a dark bill with a yellow base. When not feeding, small groups sit around in trees or fly between herds with their starling-like flight. Occurs in thornveld and broadleafed woodland.

Cape Sugarbird   ♂ 44 cm, ♀ 25 cm

The male is an easily identified bird with its combination of an *extremely long and wispy tail, long decurved bill, greyish-brown upperparts and speckled drab underparts with a bright lemon vent and undertail coverts*. The female and imm. are similar to the male and although they have long tails, these are never quite as long as the male's. In courtship and display the male dances in mid-air with wings flapping vigorously and his long tail partially spread as he repeatedly flicks it over his back. Found in fynbos, particularly in stands of proteas.

A WEAVING

ROY JOHANNESSON

Above left: male
Left: female

Malachite Sunbird   ♂ 25 cm, ♀ 15 cm

Male

G. CUBITT

Female

ROY JOHANNESSON

The *largest sunbird* in the region and the only one with an *all-metallic green plumage with long tail projections*. The male in 'eclipse' plumage loses his green sheen for a short period and then resembles the female. The female is olive-brown above and has yellowish underparts but is distinguished by her large size and long, decurved bill. The male's call is a high-pitched ringing 'zing-zing'. Occurs in fynbos, protea- and aloe-covered slopes, and mountain scrub.

117

Orangebreasted Sunbird ♂ 15 cm, ♀ 12 cm

Male

Female

The only small sunbird in the region to have pointed tail projections. The head is an iridescent green and blue, the back a dull olive, and the *breast and belly bright orange*. In the fynbos habitat, the female could be confused only with the female Lesser Doublecollared Sunbird but is noticeably larger and is a more uniform olive-green above and below. When breeding, the male makes himself conspicuous by sitting on an exposed perch and singing his short buzzy song. Inhabits fynbos and flowering aloe stands.

Marico Sunbird 14 cm

Male

Female

Unlike many other sunbirds that have scarlet bands across the breast, the male of this species has an *iridescent purple band* that contrasts with the black belly. The head and back are a metallic iridescent greenish-blue and the bill is long and decurved. The female is a drab olive-brown above with paler, streaked underparts and poses complex identification problems with many other similar female sunbirds; however, her long, robust and decurved bill is the distinguishing feature. Frequents thornveld and dry broadleafed woodland.

118

Lesser Doublecollared Sunbird 12 cm

Male   Female

The *smallest of the sunbirds that have a scarlet breast band*. Confusion arises with the Greater Doublecollared Sunbird from which it can be distinguished by its *smaller size, shorter and finer decurved bill, and a much narrower scarlet breast band*. The female differs from the female Greater Doublecollared Sunbird by the smaller bill character and from the female Orange-breasted Sunbird by being greyer on the underparts. The call is a harsh 'chee-chee'. Found in coastal scrub, fynbos and forest edge.

Greater Doublecollared Sunbird 14 cm

Male   Female

Within its range likely to be confused only with the Lesser Doublecollared Sunbird from which it can be distinguished as it is considerably *larger, has a longer, thicker bill and a broader scarlet breast band*. The females of both species are olive and dark brown but the female Greater Doublecollared is noticeably greener on the underparts and has a longer, heavier bill. It is active and restless, flitting about and uttering a harsh 'tchut-tchut-tchut'. Occurs in stands of proteas and aloes in mountainous terrain.

Whitebellied Sunbird 11 cm

Left: male
Above: female

A very small sunbird and the only one in the region to have a *bottle green head and back, and a white belly*. The female is nondescript and looks like a small grey warbler with a white belly, but the long decurved bill confirms that it is a sunbird. The male is conspicuous during the breeding season when he perches high to deliver his fast, buzzy song. At other times, they keep to forest edge and thicket.

Scarletchested Sunbird 15 cm

Male

Female

A large, chunky sunbird, the male is unmistakable: it has a *matt black body and bright scarlet breast*. At close range the iridescent blue flecks on the scarlet breast can be seen. The female resembles the female Black Sunbird but has *more mottled underparts* and *lacks the buff moustachial stripes* of that species. The male is bold and conspicuous, chasing other birds from his territory. The song is a loud 'cheeup-chup-toop-toop' whistle. Occurs in mixed dry and moist woodland, thornveld and suburbia.

Black Sunbird 15 cm

N. MYBURGH

J.L. VILJOEN

Although this sunbird is the same length as the Scarletchested Sunbird, it is more *slender* and has a neater, more compact body shape. This appearance, together with its longer tail, should help in identifying the confusingly similar females of these two species. The male is easily distinguished by his *matt black plumage* which is relieved only by an *iridescent greenish-violet patch on the throat and shoulder, and a bronze-green forehead*. These patches are not easy to see unless the bird is in direct sunlight. The female closely resembles the female Scarletchested Sunbird but has very obvious buff moustachial stripes and is paler and less streaked below. Found in evergreen, coastal and riverine forest, and suburbia.

Above left: male
Left: female

Cape White-eye 12 cm

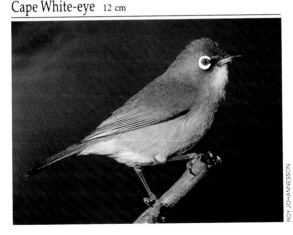

ROY JOHANNESSON

The plumage of this warbler-like bird varies from region to region but it is usually *olive-green above, greyish below* and has a diagnostic *ring of white feathering around the eye*. They are noisy and active birds, commonly found in groups as they work their way through the undergrowth or high up in the canopy. They are inveterate members of bird parties and the soft 'tweee-tuuu-twee-twee' call is continually repeated as they keep contact. Found in a wide range of habitats, including gardens.

Redbilled Buffalo Weaver 24 cm

Male

 The only large, *black, sparrow-like bird* in the region. It has a robust red bill and in flight shows white patches in the primary feathers. The female and imm. are browner versions of the male. Feeds mostly on the ground; when disturbed, groups will fly up into trees. Their nests are large, untidy bundles of thorny sticks, placed in trees and windmills. Occurs in dry thornveld and broadleafed woodland.

Whitebrowed Sparrow-weaver 19 cm

A plump, short-tailed bird with a *broad white eyebrow stripe which runs from behind the eye, a conspicuous white rump* (visible in flight), and a white wing stripe. It occurs in groups, usually near the nesting or roosting trees. The nests, many of which are placed in a single tree, are untidy bundles of straw. The birds' loud and liquid 'cheeoop-preeoo-chop' call is given from these colonies; a harsher 'chik-chik' alarm call is also given. Found in thornveld and dry, scrubby river courses.

House Sparrow 14 cm

Male   Female

Its close association with man makes this possibly the best
known bird in the region. The male has a *grey crown and
rump, black bib, pale cheeks, chestnut mantle and a white
wing bar*. The female is a drab greyish-brown with a streaked mantle,
a buffish eyebrow stripe and paler off-white underparts. A displaying
male will droop his wings, cock his tail and hold his head back as he
hops around a female. Rarely absent from human habitation; has col-
onized remote farms and offshore islands of the region.

Cape Sparrow 15 cm

Male   Female

A larger and plumper bird than the House Sparrow, the
male is also more distinctively marked with a *bold black
and white head pattern*. The female has a chestnut mantle
and a shadow impression of the male's head pattern. It has adapted to
human habitation but is frequently found in remote areas, far from
urban development. Occurs mostly in small groups or pairs but at
times forms large flocks and joins parties of bishops, weavers and
queleas feeding on old grain fields and crops.

Southern Greyheaded Sparrow 15 cm

W.R. TARBOTON

An unobtrusive sparrow which has a *grey head and under-parts*, a *chestnut mantle and rump*, and a *white wing bar*. Might be mistaken for the female House Sparrow but the very obvious grey head should eliminate confusion. Occurs in the vicinity of farm buildings and yards where it associates with Cape and House Sparrows but it is more often seen in open woodland, particularly on dead trees in which it can nest. Occurs in mixed woodland and suburbia in some areas.

Yellowthroated Sparrow 15 cm

W.P. STANFORD

Frequently mistaken for Whitebrowed Sparrow-weaver because of the *broad buffy eyebrow stripe* which begins just above the eye and can appear very white in some lights and plumages. However, the Yellowthroated Sparrow is very much smaller, lacks a white rump and has buff underparts. This species can also resemble a female House Sparrow but its eyebrow stripe is broader, it has two buff wing bars and would seldom be found in the same habitat. Occurs in small groups. Inhabits thornveld, broad-leafed woodland and riverine bush.

124

Scalyfeathered Finch 10 cm

W.R TARBOTON

When in flight, this tiny finch appears as a grey blur but, when seen at rest, the contrasting *black and white malar stripes, freckled black and white forehead and white fringed wing and tail feathers* make identification easy. It feeds mostly on the ground and it is not easy to see but when flushed it will settle on bushes in an exposed position. The call is an indistinct 'chizz-chizz', given by birds in flight. Found in dry thornveld, and at cattle enclosures, watering troughs and around farm buildings.

Thickbilled Weaver 18 cm

Male   Female

N BRICKELL   A. WEAVING

This large weaver is the only one with such a *massive, thick bill,* and *dark brown plumage relieved only by white patches in the wings* and a *white forehead.* The female appears markedly different, being brown above and paler and heavily streaked below, but still shows the large bill. Small flocks are often seen as they fly to and from their roosts, giving their 'tweek-tweek' call. In flight, the males' white wing patches appear translucent. Occurs in evergreen and coastal forests, and in reedbeds.

Spottedbacked Weaver 17 cm

The male in breeding plumage is the *only black-faced weaver to have a yellow and black speckled back*. The race that occurs in the north has the same extent of black on the head as the Masked Weaver but the spotted back should help distinguish the species. When not breeding the male loses his bright yellow plumage and attains the drab greenish and olive colour of the female and imm. It is then exceedingly difficult to differentiate from other weavers in similar plumage. Breeds, sometimes in large colonies, in trees overhanging water.

Above left: breeding male
Left: female

Cape Weaver 17 cm

Most likely to be confused with the Yellow Weaver from which it is distinguished by being *larger*, less brilliant yellow in colour, having an *orange- or rust-coloured wash over the face, and by having a cream, not red eye*. The non-breeding male resembles the olive and yellowish female and imm. The breeding colonies are usually situated in reedbeds or in trees overhanging water. The male will hang from a completed nest and sway from side to side, flapping his wings and giving the swizzling notes typical of weavers. Found in reedbeds, agricultural lands and upland vleis.

Above left: breeding male
Left: female

Masked Weaver 15 cm

Breeding male

Female

 The breeding male can be distinguished from the male Spottedbacked Weaver by its *uniform yellowish-green back* and by the *greater extent of black on the head*, especially on the forehead. The non-breeding male, female and imm. are alike, having yellowish underparts and olive-brown upperparts, and are difficult to differentiate from other non-breeding weavers. It is usually found in small breeding colonies; when not breeding it forms part of mixed flocks of bishops and weavers. Occurs in thornveld, trees over water and in agricultural lands.

Lesser Masked Weaver 14 cm

Breeding male

Female

 Slightly smaller and more compact than the similar Masked Weaver, this species is easily distinguished in breeding plumage by having *more extensive black on the head*, encompassing the crown and extending on to the throat in a *rounded, not pointed bib*. This species further differs from the Masked Weaver in all plumages by having a *pale, not red eye* and *bluish, not brown legs and feet*. Colonial breeder in trees overhanging rivers and dams, and in reedbeds. Out of the breeding season, it forms mixed flocks with other weavers.

Yellow Weaver 15 cm

Breeding male

Female

The male in breeding plumage is best distinguished from the breeding male Cape Weaver by its smaller size, more *vivid golden-yellow plumage*, less extensive wash of orange on the face and a *bright red, not cream eye*. The non-breeding male, and the female and imm. are similar in appearance; unlike other weavers in alternate plumage, they have a distinct pale yellow throat and breast which is sharply demarcated from the white underparts. It breeds in reedbeds, but is often seen foraging in woodland.

Redbilled Quelea 13 cm

Breeding male

Non-breeding female

The male of this small finch in breeding plumage is unmistakable with his *black face bordered with red* and his *bright red bill and legs*. The non-breeding male and female are very sparrow-like but still show the red bill and legs. The breeding female has a horn-coloured bill. This species is best known for concentrating in hundreds of thousands of birds which fly in tightly packed flocks. Occurs in mixed dry woodland, grassland and farmlands.

128

Red Bishop   14 cm

Breeding male   Female

A male Red Bishop in breeding plumage can easily be identified by the combination of its *bright orange and black plumage*. The female, imm. and non-breeding male are not easily distinguished from the similarly plumaged Golden Bishop but this species appears darker and has more heavily streaked underparts. The male performs a spectacular display flight in which he fluffs out his feathers and, with rapid wing beats, whizzes to and fro like a giant bumble-bee. Found in reedbeds adjoining fresh water, and agricultural lands.

Golden Bishop   12 cm

Most often seen together with widows and weavers in very large mixed flocks when all the birds appear as unidentifiable 'little brown jobs' with mottled and streaked brown and buff plumages. This species most closely resembles the Red Bishop in this obscure plumage but is noticeably smaller, more compact and is paler overall with reduced streaking on the breast and flanks. The male in breeding plumage is easily identified by his *yellow and black coloration* and his *unusual bumble-bee-like flight* over his territory. Found in reedbeds and grasses near water, and arable crops and grasslands.

Breeding male above,
female below

Yellowrumped Widow 15 cm

ROY JOHANNESSON

P. J. GINN

Breeding male   Female

The predominantly black plumage of the male widow birds' breeding plumage gives them their name, but all show some diagnostic yellow or red markings. This species has a *bright yellow rump and lower back* and a *yellow shoulder patch*. The female shows a dull yellow rump which distinguishes her from all other female widow birds. The male in non-breeding plumage resembles the female but, in flight, shows a yellow rump and shoulder patch. Frequents damp grassy areas, bracken-covered mountain valleys and fynbos.

Redshouldered Widow 19 cm

Only two widow birds in the region have red shoulder patches: this species and the Longtailed Widow. This species is far smaller and the breeding male does not have a very long tail. Also, the *red shoulder of this species has no broad buff stripe on the lower edge*. In non-breeding plumage, the male is easily distinguished by his red shoulder patch but the female lacks any obvious field characters. Occurs over reedbeds, damp grasslands and in sugarcane plantations.

N BRICKELL

Breeding male

Whitewinged Widow 15-19 cm

Breeding male

Female

Could possibly be confused with the Yellowrumped Widow in breeding and non-breeding plumages but this species *lacks any yellow on the back or rump* and the *yellow shoulder patch is bordered by white* on the lower edge. The male in non-breeding plumage retains the yellow and white shoulder patch. The female lacks the dull yellow rump of the female Yellowrumped Widow. During the non-breeding season, flocks in flight are easily recognized by their diagnostic yellow and white shoulder patches. Found in damp grassy areas and in reedbeds.

Redcollared Widow 15 cm, plus 25 cm tail

Breeding male

Female

The breeding male resembles a diminutive Longtailed Widow and at a distance they might be confused, but this species lacks the red shoulder. At closer range the red crescentic marking on the throat can easily be seen. The non-breeding male, the female and imm. are very similar to the plainly coloured bishops and other widows but this species shows a boldly striped head and plain buffy underparts. It is one of the few species that has adapted to the sugarcane belt in the east of the region.

131

Longtailed Widow ♂ 19 cm, plus 40 cm tail; ♀ 16 cm

Above: non-breeding
Left: Breeding male

The breeding male is unmistakable with his *exceptionally long tail and bright red shoulder patches bordered with buff.* Out of the breeding season, the tail is lost and the plumage becomes mottled brown and buff but he retains the red shoulder character. The female is the largest of all the female widows, has a rounded wing, floppy flight and shows a dark underwing. When displaying, the male flies with the long tail dangling and held spread, and his wings flapping with jerky circular movements. Inhabits open grasslands and damp grassy valleys.

Pintailed Whydah 12 cm, plus 22 cm tail

Above: male
Below: female

The breeding male is unmistakable with his *pied plumage and very long black tail.* The female and non-breeding male are a *drab, mottled brown and buff with dark stripes on the head* but the male in this plumage still shows a red bill. In this obscure plumage they can be distinguished from the similarly marked bishops by the dark streaks on the buff head and by the white outertail feathers. During the breeding season the male performs a low aerial display flight in which he dances and bobs in front of females. Found in grasslands, and in suburbia.

Shafttailed Whydah   12 cm, plus 22 cm tail

Where the ranges of the Pintailed and Shafttailed Whydah overlap, it can be difficult to distinguish between them in non-breeding plumage. The males in breeding plumage are easily differentiated as the Shafttailed has *warm buff underparts and collar and the tail has diagnostic spatulate tips*. The non-breeding male and female are slightly paler and have fainter head markings than the similarly plumaged Pintailed Whydah. The male has a bounding and bobbing display flight. Occurs in grassy areas in dry thornveld and broadleafed woodland.

N BRICKELL

Left: breeding male

Blue Waxbill   13 cm

W.R. TARBOTON

W.G. McILLERON

Male   Female

A small, *pale brownish* waxbill which has a diagnostic *powder blue face and breast*. The female is paler than the male with less blue on the face and underparts. It feeds on the ground; when disturbed it flies into low areas of bush to hide and gives its soft 'weep-weep' call. Usually occurs in pairs or small flocks and in drier areas frequently visits waterholes or livestock drinking troughs. Occurs in dry areas of mixed woodlands and thornveld.

133

Violeteared Waxbill 15 cm

N BRICKELL

The most colourful of the waxbills, the male has a *cinnamon body, iridescent violet ear patches* (diagnostic), *a bright blue rump and red eyes and bill*. The female and imm. are far paler but still show the diagnostic violet ear patches and the blue rump. It occurs in pairs or small family parties and is secretive except when it arrives to drink at waterholes and troughs, when it mixes freely with other waxbills and weavers. Frequents dry thornveld, rivercourses and grassy roadsides.

Above: male
Below: female

W.R. TARBOTON

Bronze Mannikin 9 cm

A WILSON

Adult

N BRICKELL

Immature

This *tiny, black-headed bird* is easily identified by its *brown, black and white plumage*. The bronze-green shoulder is not easy to see unless the bird is in sunlight but the barred brown flanks contrast clearly with the white breast. The imm. is completely dun brown with a small yellow gape: in this plumage the imm. would be accompanied by adults. Small groups are often seen huddled side by side on a perch. Found in grassy areas in woodlands, forest edges and damp regions.

134

Yelloweyed Canary 12 cm

A. WILSON

Where their ranges overlap, the Yelloweyed Canary could be confused with the male Yellow Canary but this species has a distinct *black line through the eye*, a *black moustachial stripe* and a grey nape. These features tend to emphasize the yellow around the eye which the Yellow Canary never shows. It is distinguished from the Bully Canary by being smaller and by having a less robust bill. The imm. is a more buffy yellow below. Found in thornveld, mixed woodland, forest edge and in suburbia.

Blackthroated Canary 11 cm

N. BRICKELL

A small, nondescript grey and brown canary which has a diagnostic *black speckled throat*. It also has a *bright yellow rump* which contrasts with the drab plumage and is conspicuous as the bird takes flight. An active and shy canary, very quick to take flight, it occurs in groups or small flocks. Frequents dry woodland, thornveld and scrub.

Cape Canary 13 cm

Adult

Immature

The lilting, tinkling call note, unlike that of any other canary, is often the first indication of this species' presence. Small groups are usually encountered as they feed on grasses and other seeding plants; when flushed, they show their *grey and green plumage*. It differs from the Yelloweyed Canary by *lacking that species' facial markings*. The imm. resembles the female Yellow Canary but has yellowish-green, not white streaked underparts. Frequents fynbos and mountainous terrain.

Bully Canary 15 cm

This is the *largest of the 'yellow' canaries* and in all plumages it shows a much *heavier, more robust bill*. The dark southern birds can be told from the Yellow and Yelloweyed Canaries by their larger size, chunkier bill and the greenish wash across the breast. The more vivid northern birds are distinguished from the Yellow Canary by the more massive bill and by lacking a contrasting yellow rump. An inconspicuous canary, it occurs in pairs or small groups. Found in scrub, woodlands and coastal scrub.

Yellow Canary 13 cm

Male   Female

The 'yellow' canary of the more arid regions. It has a dark form which might be mistaken for a Bully or Yelloweyed Canary but it *lacks the greenish breast band of the former and the black facial markings* of the latter. It is a much *brighter golden-yellow* than the pale form Bully Canary. The female and imm. differ from the female Cape Canary by having whitish, not yellowish-green underparts streaked with brown. An inhabitant of Karoo and coastal scrub, thornveld and mountainous scrub.

Goldenbreasted Bunting 16 cm

The *black and white striped head, chestnut mantle and yellow-orange breast* are diagnostic in this bunting. The female and imm. are duller versions of the male. It often reveals its presence by giving a nasal, buzzy 'zzhrrrr' call or its song, a varied 'weechee-weechee-weechee', from within the canopy of a tree. Feeds on the ground; when flushed, will fly a short distance, displaying its white outertail, white wing bars and chestnut back. Found in thornveld, broadleafed woodland and exotic plantations.

Cape Bunting 16 cm

ROY JOHANNESSON

The head pattern of this bird resembles that of the Golden-breasted Bunting but is grey and black striped. This, combined with the *grey breast and chestnut shoulder*, render it easily identified. In its rocky and sandy terrain this small bird shuffles around on the ground searching for food; when disturbed, it will dash for cover behind a rock or bush. The call is a nasal, ascending 'zzzoo-zeh-zee-zee' and the song, given from a prominent rock, consists of a series of chirping notes.

Larklike Bunting 14 cm

A. WILSON

It is the *lack of any definite field characters* in this *drab and dowdy* bird that points to its identification. It might be mistaken for a lark but it exhibits typical bunting behaviour, hopping over stones and grubbing around for seeds on bare ground. It is often flushed from road verges. It occurs in the drier areas and commonly frequents waterholes and livestock drinking troughs, sometimes in large numbers. Its contact call is a short 'tuc-tuc'. Found in dry rocky valleys, desert edge and open plains.

138

Birding etiquette

Once you are equipped with a pair of binoculars, a notebook and a field guide, you are on the road to birding and no other licence is required. Access to most game and nature reserves, wildlife sanctuaries and wilderness areas is allowed if the necessary permits are arranged prior to the visit, and any admission fees paid. Most other birding areas are on privately owned land and, although birding from the road into these areas is acceptable, it is not advisable to go across the veld unless you have sought permission from the landowner. Enter fields through gates or by climbing carefully through and not over a fence.

The ever-increasing number of birders is placing pressure on the better known birding areas and, to avoid being denied access, birders should observe a simple code of etiquette. In their innocent pursuit birders can disturb and harm the very things that have taken their interest. Watching a flock of terns or roosting waders on a beach might seem harmless enough but if you put them to flight you are directly causing a disturbance. This is tolerable if you do it only once, but repeatedly disturbing flocks causes distress and the birds subsequently move away altogether – this often happens if there is more than one birder in the area. Making any kind of close approach to breeding colonies of birds such as weavers, bishops, herons and seabirds can cause incalculable harm and may even result in the entire colony disbanding and deserting, with a total breeding failure in that season. Viewing birds in this situation is simple if a quiet and careful approach is made or, even better, if you use a spotting scope and thus avoid too close an approach altogether.

It is easy to recognize the situations in which birds will flush. They become very agitated, sometimes giving off alarm notes, and will begin wing stretching. Respect these signals and leave the vicinity. General disturbance of any breeding birds should be avoided – with experience you will be able to tell if a bird is holding a territory and actively nesting. A nesting bird or a bird with young may feign injury, give alarm calls, or dive bomb an intruder in an effort to distract attention away from its nest or young. When you recognize these signals it is best to limit your time in the immediate area in case you cause the birds to desert.

A technique which is being employed more frequently is that of using a tape recording of a bird's call or song to entice the bird into the open for better viewing. This practice is useful for attracting the more furtive species and, in particular, nocturnal owls and nightjars. It does not do any harm if done very infrequently but most certainly will if the bird is repeatedly lured to a tape recording. A bird responding to a taped call is doing so to seek out an invader to its territory, and if it cannot see the intruder to chase it away, it will inevitably become confused. If continually lured to a tape, the bird defending its territory will eventually abandon the area.

The key to 'unobtrusive' birding is to have the bird's interests in mind. Remember all the time that the habitat in which you are watching the bird is fragile: take care not to damage it or to disturb the area.

Actively involve yourself in a local or national conservation society and draw their attention to areas near you that need conserving or that are being disturbed or developed. If added up on a national scale, the small areas of natural habitat which are rapidly being destroyed and cleared for development would cover a vast area.

Glossary of terms

Alien A bird which is not indigenous to the area.

Call Short notes given by males and females for alarm and contact purposes (*see* Song).

Cap Area encompassing the forehead and crown.

Casque A helmet or helmet-like process on the bill.

Cere Coloured bare skin at the base of the upper mandible (in raptors).

Colonial Associating in close proximity, either while roosting, feeding or nesting.

Crest Elongated feathers on the forehead, crown or nape.

Cryptic Pertaining to camouflage coloration.

Decurved Curving downwards.

Display A pattern of behaviour in which the bird attracts attention while it is defending territory or courting a female, for example.

Endemic Restricted to a certain region.

Eye-ring Circle of coloured feathers immediately behind the eye.

Feral Species that have escaped from captivity and now live in the wild.

Flush To rouse and put to flight.

Immature A bird that has moulted its juvenile plumage but has not yet attained full adult plumage.

Juvenile The first full-feathered plumage of a young bird.

Migrant A species that undertakes long-distance flights between its wintering and breeding areas.

Moustachial stripes Lines running from the base of the bill to the sides of the throat (*see* malar region *in illustration*).

Parasitize When a bird lays its eggs in the nest of another species for the purposes of incubation.

Plumage Feathering of a kind.

Primaries The outermost major flight feathers of the wing.

Resident A bird that occurs throughout the year in a region and is not known to undertake migration.

Roost To sleep or rest, either in flocks or singly.

Secondaries Flight feathers of the wing, adjoining the primary feathers.

Shield Bare patch of skin at the base of the bill and on the forehead. Often brightly coloured.

Song A series of notes given by the male to proclaim his territory (*see* Call).

Summer visitor A bird that is absent from the region during winter.

Territory An area that a bird establishes and subsequently defends from others.

Vent Area from the belly to the undertail coverts.

Parts of a bird

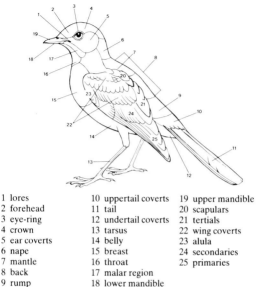

1 lores	10 uppertail coverts	19 upper mandible
2 forehead	11 tail	20 scapulars
3 eye-ring	12 undertail coverts	21 tertials
4 crown	13 tarsus	22 wing coverts
5 ear coverts	14 belly	23 alula
6 nape	15 breast	24 secondaries
7 mantle	16 throat	25 primaries
8 back	17 malar region	
9 rump	18 lower mandible	

Habitat

MAJOR VEGETATION ZONES OF SOUTHERN AFRICA

Thornveld and Broadleafed woodland

Desert and Semi-desert

Grasslands

Evergreen forest

Mountains

0   500 km

Fynbos

Temperate forest

The map of the region (above) shows the major vegetation zones mentioned in the text. Bird distribution is contained by, and in many cases, restricted to specialized habitats within these zones.

Further reading

The following books may be of interest to those wishing to learn more about birds and bird-watching.

Berruti, A., and Sinclair, J.C. 1983. *Where to Watch Birds in Southern Africa*. Struik Publishers, Cape Town.

Ginn, P., McIlleron, W.G., and Milstein, P. 1989. *The Complete Book of Southern African Birds*. Struik Winchester, Cape Town.

Harrison, P. 1983. *Seabirds: An Identification Guide*. Croom Helm, London.

Heinzel, H., Fitter, R., and Parslow, J. 1972. *The Birds of Britain and Europe with North Africa and the Middle East*. Collins, London.

King, B., Woodcock, M., and Dickinson, E.C. 1975. *A Field Guide to the Birds of South East Asia*. Collins, London.

Maclean, G.L. 1984 (5th edition). *Roberts' Birds of Southern Africa*. The Trustees of the John Voelcker Bird Book Fund, Cape Town.

Newman, K.B. 1987. *Birds of the Kruger National Park*. Southern Book Publishers, Johannesburg.

Newman, K.B. 1983. *Newman's Birds of Southern Africa*. Macmillan South Africa, Johannesburg.

Pickford, P. and B., and Tarboton, W. 1989. *Southern African Birds of Prey*. Struik Publishers, Cape Town.

Robbins, C.S., Bruun, B., and Zimm, H.S. 1966. *A Guide to the Field Identification: Birds of North America*. Golden Press, New York.

Sinclair, I., and Goode, D. 1986. *Struik Pocket Guide Series: Birds of Prey*. Struik Publishers, Cape Town.

Sinclair, I., and Goode, D. 1987. *Struik Pocket Guide Series: Highveld Birds*. Struik Publishers, Cape Town.

Sinclair, I., Meakin, P., and Goode, D. 1990. *Struik Pocket Guide Series: Common Birds*. Struik Publishers, Cape Town.

Sinclair, J.C., Mendelsohn, J.M., and Johnson, P. 1981. *Everyone's Guide to South African Birds*. CNA, Johannesburg.

Steyn, P. 1982. *Birds of Prey of Southern Africa*. David Philip, Cape Town.

Index

Figures in **bold type** indicate the main species entry

Albatross, Blackbrowed **7**, 8
　Yellownosed **8**
Apalis, Barthroated **99**
　Yellowbreasted 99, **100**
Avocet **47**

Babbler, Arrowmarked **89**
Barbet, Blackcollared **74**, 75
　Crested **76**
　Pied **75**, 75
　Redfronted Tinker **75**, 75, 76
　Yellowfronted Tinker 75, **76**
Bateleur **27**
Batis, Cape **104**
　Chinspot 104, **105**
Bee-eater, European **68**
　Little **68**
　Whitefronted **69**
Bishop, Golden **129**, 129
　Red **129**, 129
Bokmakierie **111**
Boubou, Southern **109**
Bulbul, Blackeyed **89**, 90
　Cape **90**, 90
　Redeyed 89, **90**, 90
Bunting, Cape **138**
　Goldenbreasted **137**, 138
　Larklike **138**
Bustard, Kori **38**
Buzzard, Jackal **29**
　Steppe **29**, 29

Canary, Blackthroated **135**
　Bully 135, **136**, 137
　Cape **136**, 137
　Yelloweyed **135**, 136
　Yellow 135, 136, **137**, 137
Chat, Anteating **94**
　Familiar **94**
　Mountain **93**
Cisticola, Fantailed **101**
　Greybacked **102**
　Rattling **102**
Coot, Redknobbed **38**
Cormorant, Cape 9, **12**
　Reed 12, **13**
　Whitebreasted **12**, 12, 13
Coucal, Burchell's **62**
Crake, Black **36**
Crane, Blue **36**
　Crowned **35**
Crombec, Longbilled **100**
Crow, Black **86**
　House **86**
　Pied 86, **87**
Cuckoo, Black **61**, 61
　Diederik **62**
　Jacobin **61**, 61
　Klaas's 62
　Redchested **60**
Cuckooshrike, Black **84**

Dabchick **7**
Darter 12, **13**, 13
Dikkop, Spotted **48**
Dove, Cape Turtle 54, **55**, 55
　Greenspotted **56**
　Laughing **55**
　Namaqua **56**
　Redeyed **54**, 55
Drongo, Forktailed 61, **85**
Duck, Whitefaced **21**
　Yellowbilled **22**, 22, 23

Eagle, African Fish **28**
　Blackbreasted Snake **26**
　Longcrested **28**
Egret, Cattle **15**
　Little **15**

Falcon, Eastern Redfooted **32**
　Lanner **31**
Finch, Scalyfeathered **125**
Finchlark, Greybacked **80**
Flamingo, Greater **20**, 20
　Lesser **20**, 20
Flycatcher, Fiscal **104**, 108
　Marico **103**
　Paradise **105**
Francolin, Cape **34**
　Crested **33**
　Swainson's **34**

Gallinule, Purple **37**, 37
Gannet, Cape 9, **11**
Godwit, Bartailed **46**, 46
Goose, Egyptian **21**
　Spurwinged **19**
Goshawk, African **30**, 30, 31
　Gabar **30**, 31
　Pale Chanting **31**
Greenshank **45**
Guineafowl, Helmeted **35**
Gull, Greyheaded **49**, 50
　Hartlaub's 49, **50**
　Kelp 7, 48, **49**

Hamerkop **16**
Helmetshrike, White **112**
Heron, Blackheaded **14**, 14
　Grey **14**, 14
Honeyguide, Lesser **77**
Hoopoe **70**, 75
Hornbill, Grey **72**, 73
　Ground **74**
　Redbilled **73**, 73
　Southern Yellowbilled 72, **73**, 73
　Trumpeter **72**

Ibis, Hadedah **18**
　Sacred **18**

Jacana, African **39**

Kestrel, Lesser 32, **33**
　Rock **32**, 33
Kingfisher, Brownhooded 65, **66**
　Malachite **65**
　Pied **66**
　Striped **67**
　Woodland **65**, 66
Kite, Blackshouldered **26**
　Yellowbilled **25**
Korhaan, Black **39**

Lark, Redcapped **80**
　Rufousnaped **78**
　Sabota **79**
　Spikeheeled **79**
Longclaw, Orangethroated **107**
　Yellowthroated **108**
Lourie, Grey **58**

143

Knysna **57**, 58
Purplecrested 57, **58**

Mannikin, Bronze **134**
Martin, Rock **83**
Moorhen **37**, 38
Mousebird, Redfaced 59, **60**
  Speckled **59**, 59
  Whitebacked **59**, 59
Myna, Indian **113**

Nightjar, Fierynecked **64**

Oriole, Blackheaded **85**
Ostrich **6**
Owl, African Scops **64**
  Barn **63**
  Spotted Eagle **63**
Oxpecker, Redbilled **116**
Oystercatcher, African Black **40**

Parrot, Brownheaded **57**
Pelican, Pinkbacked 10, **11**
  White **10**, 11
Penguin, Jackass **6**
Petrel, Pintado **8**
  Whitechinned 9, 9, 11
Pigeon, Feral **53**
  Rameron **54**
  Rock **53**
Pipit, Grassveld **107**
Plover, Blacksmith **43**
  Crowned **42**
  Grey **42**
  Kittlitz's 40, **41**
  Threebanded **41**
  Whitefronted **40**, 41
Pochard, Southern **24**
Prinia, Spotted **103**
Prion, Broadbilled **10**
Puffback **110**

Quelea, Redbilled **128**

Raven, Whitenecked **87**, 87
Robin, Cape **96**
  Heuglin's **97**
  Karoo **97**
  Natal **95**
  Whitebrowed **96**
Roller, European **69**
  Lilacbreasted 69, **70**

Sandgrouse, Namaqua **52**
Sandpiper, Common **44**, 44
  Curlew **45**
  Wood **44**
Secretarybird **24**
Shearwater, Sooty **9**, 9
Shoveler, Cape **23**
Shrike, Crimsonbreasted **110**
  Fiscal 104, **108**, 109
  Redbacked **109**
Skua, Subantarctic **48**
Sparrow, Cape **123**, 124
  House **123**, 123, 124
  Southern Greyheaded **124**
  Yellowthroated **124**
Sparrow-weaver, Whitebrowed **122**, 124
Spoonbill, African **19**

Starling, Blackbellied **115**, 115
  European **112**, 114
  Glossy **115**, 115
  Pied **113**
  Plumcoloured **114**
  Redwinged **116**
  Wattled **114**
Stilt, Blackwinged **47**
Stonechat 93, **95**
Stork, Abdim's **17**
  Marabou **17**
  White **16**, 17
Sugarbird, Cape **117**
Sunbird, Black 120, **121**
  Greater Doublecollared **119**, 119
  Lesser Doublecollared 118, **119**, 119
  Malachite **117**
  Marico **118**
  Orangebreasted **118**, 119
  Scarletchested **120**, 121
  Whitebellied **120**
Swallow, European **81**
  Greater Striped **81**, 82
  Lesser Striped 81, **82**, 82
  Redbreasted **83**
  South African Cliff **82**
  Whitethroated **84**

Tchagra, Blackcrowned **111**
Teal, Cape **22**
  Redbilled 22, **23**
Tern, Caspian **50**, 51
  Common **51**
  Swift **51**
  Whitewinged **52**
Thrush, Cape Rock **92**
  Groundscraper **92**
  Kurrichane **91**, 91
  Olive **91**, 91
Tit, Ashy **88**
  Southern Black **88**
Titbabbler **98**
Trogon, Narina **67**
Turnstone **43**

Vulture, Whitebacked **25**

Wagtail, African Pied **106**, 106
  Cape **106**
Warbler, African Sedge **99**
  Bleating **101**
  Cape Reed **98**
Waxbill, Blue **133**
  Violeteared **134**
Weaver, Cape **126**, 128
  Lesser Masked **127**
  Masked 126, **127**, 127
  Redbilled Buffalo **122**
  Spottedbacked **126**, 127
  Thickbilled **125**
  Yellow 126, **128**
Wheatear, Capped **93**
Whimbrel **46**
White-eye, Cape **121**
Whydah, Pintailed **132**, 133
  Shafttailed **133**
Widow, Longtailed 130, 131, **132**
  Redcollared **131**
  Redshouldered **130**
  Whitewinged **131**
  Yellowrumped **130**, 131
Woodhoopoe, Redbilled **71**, 71
  Scimitarbilled **71**
Woodpecker, Cardinal **78**
  Goldentailed **77**, 78